TEN WALKS
THAT CHANGED THE WORLD

Walks into Shropshire's Industrial Past

Kate and Keith Pybus

EXPLORING SHROPSHIRE
with
Shropshire Books

EXPLORING SHROPSHIRE

TEN WALKS THAT CHANGED THE WORLD forms part of a series of books and leaflets on walking published by Shropshire Books known as **EXPLORING SHROPSHIRE**. For other titles in the series see page 71.

Front cover: Chirk aquaduct and viaduct. Photograph by Gordon Dickins.

ISBN: 0-903802-69-4

The maps are based on the 1992 Ordnance Survey 1:25,000 mapping with permission of the Controller of her Majesty's Stationery Office
© Crown Copyright.

© Kate and Keith Pybus 1996

Cover and Book design: Daywell Designs

Maps: Reprographics

Illustrations: Kathryn Green and Malcolm Newton

Managing Editor: Helen Sample

Published by Shropshire Books, the publishing Division of the Information and Community Services Department of Shropshire County Council.

Printed in Great Britain by Midland Printing

CONTENTS

Exploration and Discovery

Where was the first passenger-carrying locomotive made?

Where was Europe's richest lead mine?

Where was the world's first sky-scraper designed and built?

Where did Thomas Minton design the Willow Pattern plate?

Where did they find the stone for the portal of 10 Downing Street?

Where was England's highest coal mine?

For us the ideal walk combines beautiful or dramatic scenery with a goal, an adventure, something to set you thinking and talking.

Exploring our industrial past is specially satisfying. Industrial heritage sites still leave lots to the imagination. They are not too neatly packaged, there is room for scrambling around, peering under brambles. If you have an eye for beauty that is there too. The Hoffman kiln at Llanymynech is worthy of any architect.

Much has survived of the part played by the men and women of Shropshire in the Industrial Revolution. These walks combine to tell Shropshire's extraordinary story and why it changed the world. One you can trace for yourself on the ground.

Kate and Keith Pybus

ACKOWLEDGEMENTS

We met with much help on the way. Mr Lloyd at Clee Hill, who showed us round where he had begun work as a boy seventy years ago. Dave Boulter at Snailbeach, who gave us a piece of lead which we treasure. Pauline Hannigan for her help with the boatmen's brothel. George Alcock kindly allowed us to use his work on the Industrial Revolution in Shrewsbury. Nigel Jones, Dave Morris, John Newnham and Mike Watson of Shropshire County Council and the staff of libraries in Market Drayton, Church Stretton and Shrewsbury. George Baugh, who came up with the idea for the spa that never was. Andy Chandler, who knows all about the filming of Gone to Earth. To Anna, Barry, Meg, Nigel, Simon, Tony and our dog Lucy, who 'testdrove' the walks. And finally our thanks to 'EJS', who inspired in us both the love of walking.

The publishers would like to thank Malcolm Newton for his permission to use his excellent drawings of the Snailbeach mining site.

Public Transport

For those who prefer to travel to the start of a walk by public transport the Bus Information line is 0345 056785 or Rail Information line is 01743 364041. Both will give up-to-date timetable and route information for travel throughout Shropshire.

Warning

Exploration of disused mine workings can be dangerous unless you are properly equipped and have the necessary experience. If you are interested in exploring old mines, we recommend that you join the Shropshire Caving and Mining Club. Please remember that disused mines are often private property and you should always ask permission from the landowner before entering.

If you would like to join the club, write to the secretary:

Adrian Pearce,
72, Hopkins Heath,
Shawbirch
Telford
Shropshire TF5 0LZ
Tel: 01952 405369

KEY TO MAPS

- - - - - - Route of Walk
═══════════ Road
= = = = = Track/Unmetalled Road
──┼────┼── Railway
∿∿∿ River/Stream
❹ Route Information
S Stile
G Gate
KG Kissing Gate
Sp Sign Post
W Way Marker
FB Footbridge
PH Public House
⌒ ⌒ Bridge
P Parking
⬭ Pond/Lake
▦ 🏠 Buildings
♦ Church
+ Chapel
⟍⟋ Viewpoint
☼ Earthworks
▲ Triangulation Point

Rights of Way

Every care has been taken to ensure the accuracy of the maps and route descriptions. If a right of way is obstructed the facts should be reported to the Countryside Section of Shropshire County Council.

COALBROOKDALE

OS Map 1:50,000 Sheet No.127, Starting point GR: 666 037

3½ miles uphill and down dale

Such a tranquil spot for a Revolution. Abraham Darby I and his
five men began it, not with cannon, but with wide-bellied pots.
Yet they changed the world. It beat a path to their door to see the smelting
of iron with coke, the first iron rails and railway wheels, cannon
casting, and steam-engine cylinders.

The walk explores the beautiful hillsides which frame the Dale, visits the houses of masters and men, poses the moral dilemma of pub or Sabbath Walk and unveils the best view of the Iron Bridge and the Gorge.

1. Park in the Dale End Park or, if full, at the Museum of the River nearby. Go down to the Severn at the bottom of the Dale End car park, turn left and stop on the wooden bridge between the Antiques Centre and the river.

To Abraham Darby looking for somewhere to exploit his new patent for casting iron pots this looked a likely spot. A stream, the Coal brook, would drive a waterwheel to provide blast for a furnace. The steep slopes, unfit for agriculture, were covered in trees. The Buildwas monks had been smelting iron in charcoal furnaces since 1200. In 1707, compared to the pitiful state of the roads, the Severn was a motorway. At its mouth was Bristol, leading port for the New World.

When Abraham Darby's 'domestic' revolution was done, it was said "There was hardly a house or log cabin between the Penobscot and the Mississippi without the iron tea-kettle (from Coalbrookdale)". His heirs were to play an equally important part in The Industrial Revolution proper.

Retrace your steps, following the path up-stream into the park.

2. Turn right between two low wooden posts and stay on the path.

The Valley Hotel is the former home of the Maw family, owners

1

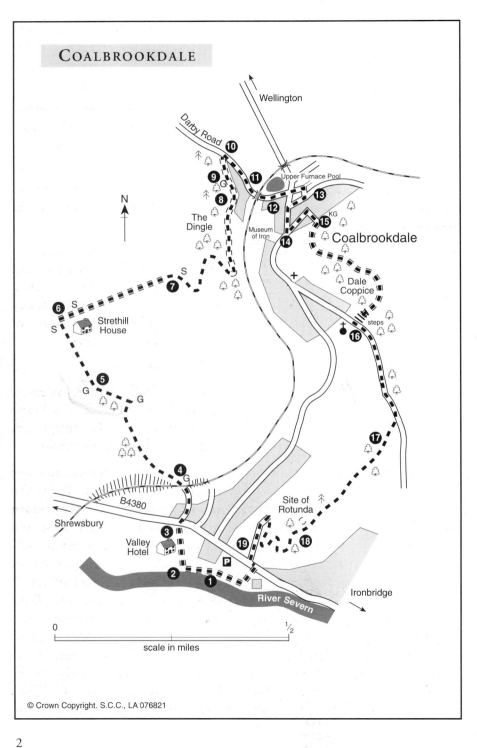

COALBROOKDALE

Wellington

Darby Road

Upper Furnace Pool

The Dingle

Museum of Iron

Coalbrookdale

KG

Dale Coppice

steps

Strethill House

N

B4380

Shrewsbury

Valley Hotel

P

Site of Rotunda

Ironbridge

River Severn

0   ½
scale in miles

© Crown Copyright. S.C.C., LA 076821

of the tile works in Jackfield.

3. Bear right and take the path between the wall and the fence. Left through the gap in the fence into the hotel car-park. Come out on to the road. Turn right and go left up Strethill Road.

4. Cross the railway which takes the coal trains to the power station. Go through the farm gate and past the houses on the right. Take the footpath straight ahead through the hawthorns. Keep the fence on your right. Through the gate and straight ahead. At the end of the wood keep on between the hawthorns and hazels, until you reach the top of the hill. Go through the gate.

Everything about the Ironbridge Gorge is spectacular. The architects of the power station have not tried to tuck away the huge 375 ft cooling towers and 670 ft chimney. The cooling towers are arranged in a sweeping arc, their 'skirts' have a strong flare and the reinforced concrete chimney is coloured pale grey to blend into the clouds and steam vapour. The great debate was about the colour of the cooling towers. Should they be given a khaki camouflage perhaps? According to one charming story, Kenneth Booth, the landscape architect, was inspired by the colour of a ploughed field, which he saw when checking the setting for the station from the top of the Wrekin. For £10,000 a tower, the reddy-pink tint was added to the concrete and the world-famous Iron Bridge gained a unique and dramatic neighbour.

5. Follow the path along the hedge, over the stile and immediately over the stile on your right.

The tramway which ran along the line of this path may have represented the first use of cast iron rails in the world.

The house behind the hedge was built in 1894 for Edward Squire. Where the path joins the track take a look at the cast-iron gate-posts, cast at the Coalbrookdale factory, of which he was the manager.

6. Follow the track.

There is another pair of gateposts further down the track, just before you reach the attractive cottage with pointed cast-iron window frames.

7. Go to the left of the oak and over the stile into The Dingle. Follow the stream, until you see some wooden steps on your left, take these and follow the path which skirts the field on your left. There are a number of paths through this piece of woodland all leading down into the Dale, do not be over-concerned where you come out, you will be able to go up the hill to the Darby houses, if you come off the hill too early. At the fork of two paths keep right. When you come to the little gate, go

through it and down the path.

8. A series of paths and brick steps meander through this former garden. It does not matter which you take, you will reach a level vehicle track. Turn left until you are looking down on the backs of two imposing houses.

The red brick one is Dale House, built for Abraham Darby I. It was completed in 1717, ten years after his arrival in Coalbrookdale, although he died before he could live in it. Abraham Darby II was brought up here. Between 1776-80, when he was planning the Iron Bridge, it was the home of Abraham Darby III.

The white-painted house next door is

Rosehill House, built in the 1730s for the manager of the Coalbrookdale Company. Later Richard Darby, son of Abraham Darby III, lived here. Visitors from all over the world came to these houses to learn about the inventions fuelling the revolutions in iron-making and transport.

9. Retrace your steps to the first garden path leading up the hill. A short way up you will see a stepped wall in the right hand boundary. Go through a rickety gate in the wooden fence and follow the path behind some houses. Take the path to your right down to the Darby Road.

Uphill to your left is The Chestnuts, home of Abraham Darby III, and the Quaker Burial Ground.

Quakers have memorial stones rather than gravestones marking individual graves. The memorial stones to the Darby family are against the wall on the left towards the top of the Burial Ground.

10. Return downhill along Darby Road.

On the right is Tea Kettle Row. There is so little flat land in Coalbrookdale that you will not find estates, or even rows, of workers' housing, just isolated terraces. This is one of the earliest, built around 1746, before the Iron Bridge and the explosive growth of the Company.

The stairs rise almost directly from the front door. Here is convincing evidence that the Quaker Ironmasters had little truck with personal show. The workers' houses are not only cheek-by-jowl with the bosses', they look down on them.

On your left is a wooden footbridge. A miniature replica of the Iron Bridge (demolished 1849) spanned the crescent-shaped Upper Furnace pool. This playful bridge would have been one of the first dozen cast iron bridges erected. Below you can see the remains of the iron ribs on the brick abutment.

11. Return to the road and go under the railway viaduct.

You are standing on the pool dam, which held back the waters of the Upper Furnace pool on your left. These reservoirs ensured year-round operation of the waterwheels which pumped the furnace bellows. Previously, iron production was pretty hit-and-miss, particularly in summer. The power of this modest stream was harnessed over and over between here and the Severn. Six pools provided the power for five ironworks.

Behind the wall on your right is the Old Furnace. Abraham Darby bought a derelict furnace where he began production with his five men. The village comprised five houses, the furnace and a forge or two. Around 1760, when the works were poised for take off, you would have seen children carrying baskets of coke, limestone and iron ore to the top of the furnace.

12. Carry on to the cross roads.

On your left is Coke Hearth. "large piles of coal burning to coke, with the intolerable stench of sulphur, approached very nearly to the idea of being in an air pump". As long as charcoal was used to smelt iron, the furnaces had to be small. The brittle fuel would not withstand a heavy charge of ore and limestone. It would collapse and the blast from the bellows could not pass through. So the mundane process with its foul smell of coal burning to coke, which took place here, lit the fuse that sparked off the Industrial Revolution.

Tea Kettle Row

You are standing on a few square yards that changed the world. Coke withstood the heavier charges. Bigger furnaces meant lower costs and bigger castings. Castings like the ribs of the Iron Bridge.

13. Cross the road to The Green. Go towards the three storey building at the end on the left.

In front of this former corn mill stood Boulton & Watt's 'Resolution' steam engine. It pumped water back from the lower pools in the Dale to the Upper Furnace Pool, so that production could continue, even when rainfall was very low. In the other corner stands the former boys' school, where the schoolboys would bake their potatoes in the hot slag from the engine. The row of cottages is called Engine Row after the 'Resolution'.

Beyond and between are two paths. A 19th century plateway ran along the lower from the Company's mines and ironworks elsewhere to those at Coalbrookdale. About 300 yards up the track is the New Pool, which drove the wheels of the corn mill and furnaces.

Back at the main road cross over and turn left.

The terrace of cottages, built in 1784 at the time of the Iron Bridge, is Carpenters' Row, where the Company's skilled pattern-makers lived. They made the wooden moulds to create the 'patterns' in the sand into which the molten iron was poured to make castings. Workers in the foundries or forges "bedew the burning sand with their streaming sweat" observed John Fletcher, the leading Methodist. It was thirsty work. And so is walking. In the interests of research we can make a stop at The Grove, once owned by the Coalbrookdale Company, or at the Coalbrookdale Inn, Camra Pub of the Year in 1995, along the road from Carpenters' Row. Church, chapel and capitalists often made common cause against the evils of drink and easy living. "When I mention drunkenness do I not name a sin most common, ...What scenes of revelling and debauchery" wrote the magistrate. Too much ale on Sunday and attendances and production suffered on Monday. There was an alternative to the pub. The Sabbath Walks, a series of paths "adorned with temples, rustic seats and other accommodation" was designed by Richard Reynolds, ironmaster and son-in-law of Abraham Darby II. The network of paths provided healthy Sunday recreation for the workers. On the steep slopes of Dale Coppice, they are quite a pipe-opener. You may be advised to restrict your biochemical research to one pint.

14. If you are tired, or have young or older members in your party, you

may wish to skip this steep climb. If so, continue down the Dale and turn left along Church Hill towards the church.

The more intrepid, should turn back towards Carpenters' Row. Take Woodside behind the cottages The middle chimney stack has cast iron chimney pots.

15. Opposite the alley from your left, go through a kissing gate uphill through the holly wood. Go up the wooden steps. At the junction of the two paths, turn left. Just before the summit, take the well-marked path down to the right. There are two paths, one plunges down very steeply for a few yards, the other is more gentle. With children or in wet weather, take the gentler incline. Soon you will come to a flight of wooden steps. Keep going down. When you see more steps on your right, take these down to the stile and Church Hill. You are opposite Holy Trinity Church.

There is much to see. Go into the churchyard through the heavy cast iron gate. The noticeboard in the porch tells you how to get hold of the key. Walk round to the right of the church. You are looking over the present Glynwed works, producing Aga and Rayburn cookers. Thus preserving the nearly three hundred year link with the first Abraham Darby's cooking pots. Between the pots and the cookers, were boilers for steam engines, the first railway wheels, early locomotives, and the Iron Bridge. Even when Coalbrookdale was supplanted as a major producer, it found a new specialist niche. Down to your left, built in 1859 of the Company's own blue bricks, is the Coalbrookdale Literary and Scientific Institute, one of the first Adult Education Colleges in the country. There was a library with 3,000 books, art exhibitions, concerts and poetry readings. Most importantly, it housed the School of Art, the means by which the Company revolutionised its business. Here they trained the designers of the fountains, statues, tables, sofas, vases and inkstands you can see in the Museum. In front of the Institute on the other side of the road was the Upper Forge pool. Its sluices, where the Coal brook still roars down to the Severn, have survived. Rich and poor are buried in the churchyard. The poorest have cast iron grave markers, the better-off cast iron tombs. At the back of the church is the grave of Abraham Darby IV. Gone is the Quaker austerity. The family tree of distinguished industrialists almost seems more important than those who are buried here. Inside the church there is a plaque to Thomas Parker, a human dynamo. He was born in the Dale in 1843, worked for the Company for twenty years, rising to Works

Manager. He developed the Parker dynamo and was responsible for the first electric tramway and underground railway. There are cast iron pew ends, and a Last Supper.

16. Leave the churchyard by the way you came in.

Down Church Hill to your left is the former Wesleyan Chapel and the terrace, known as Church or Charity Row, built for widows of the Company's workers.

Turn right up the hill.

17. Just before the bend at the top of the hill there is an opening between the iron railings and the crash barrier. Take this Sabbath Walk gently downhill. Stay on the path parallel to the Dale. The well-worn path coming up from below was once the route taken by the workers from Ironbridge to the Coalbrookdale Works. Take the path to the left. Keep straight on until you reach a wooden platform.

300 ft below is the Severn and the best view of the Gorge and the Iron Bridge. Here Reynolds built a Rotunda from which to enjoy the spectacular view. You can see the circular foundation beneath the wooden platform. The roof was supported on iron columns, but it was demolished in 1804 due to instability.

In front and below are the remains of the great Lincoln Hill limestone quarry. The quarry extended so far below ground that it too became a visitor attraction. Tours of the "prodigious caverns of limestone supported by stupendous pillars" were the highlight of 19th century fêtes. Bands played in the illuminated caverns attracting the thousands in excursion trains from Birmingham and elsewhere.

18. Take the steep flight of steps, about 140, down from the corner of the platform. Turn right and immediately left downhill. This is part of the Shropshire Way. Go down a second flight of steps. Turn right at the wall and over the stile. Follow the path until you reach the houses on the right, where the path bends back on itself. This joins up with another track which leads down to the main road known as the Wharfage.

This is the line of a plateway which carried limestone to the Coalbrookdale furnaces and to the trows at Dale End for shipment down river.

You come out on the Wharfage, opposite the Company's Severn Foundry where, between 1901 and 1917, some of the earliest gas cookers were made. It is now Merrythought, makers of cuddly toys.

19. Turn left towards the Museum of the River. Cross the road into the

museum car park. Take the riverside path from the right hand corner of the car park.

On the opposite bank you have a good view of the arches of the Severn Valley Railway viaduct. This was a mere springboard for its engineer, John Fowler. He went on to build the Forth Bridge and the Metropolitan Railway.

A last glimpse of the 'rose-red' towers and return along the riverside to Dale End car park.

A further fascinating exploration of the tramway and tub boat canals adjacent to this walk is offered by the Little Dawley/Lightmoor walk by David Gregory in 'Walks Around Telford'.

"The Iron Song 1822"

SHREWSBURY: COLEHAM TO CASTLEFIELDS

OS Map 1:50,000 Sheet No. 126, Starting point GR: 494 122

3½ miles

Visitors, and even residents might look at Shrewsbury today and ask what Industrial Revolution? But this was no Warwick or Chester, this was the county town of Shropshire. This was home to Telford and 'Merlin' Hazeldine, where even the vicars wanted to be entrepreneurs. A few miles down the river in the Ironbridge Gorge men were changing the world.

Inside the Severn's close embrace there was no room for the upstart manufacturers. But 'beyond the Pale', across the river in Coleham they had been making pots and pans since 1300. Behind or beneath today's suburban shop-fronts a great foundry, a poisonous lead works, a chapel-like sewage pumping station, a brewery and textile mill stood cheek-by-jowl. Changed the world? They even made the world's first skyscraper here.

1. Park in St Julian's Friars car park. Face the river. Leave the car park by the left-hand corner. Take the path up to the footbridge. Pause on your way across the bridge to look right.

Boulton and Watt, Rolls and Royce...; another association which deserves to be better known is that of Telford and William 'Merlin' Hazeldine. Appropriately our two 'revolutionaries' met in 1789, the year that France exploded. Their

meeting at the local freemason's lodge led to a lifelong collaboration (See Chirk Walk).

Hazeldine cast the beams and pillars for the world's first iron-framed building here at his Coleham foundry in 1797 - the first skyscraper was a Shrewsbury flax mill.

Thirty years after they met, he was entrusted with making the chains for Telford's pioneering Menai Suspension Bridge over the storm-tossed straits to Anglesey. Each chain weighed 23½ tons, each composite link was nine foot long and consisted of thirty-six bars of iron. The links were tested and assembled here. Hazeldine was aboard the first coach to rumble over Britain's largest bridge. He had forged the final link in Telford's great London-Holyhead road.

For forty years Hazeldine was

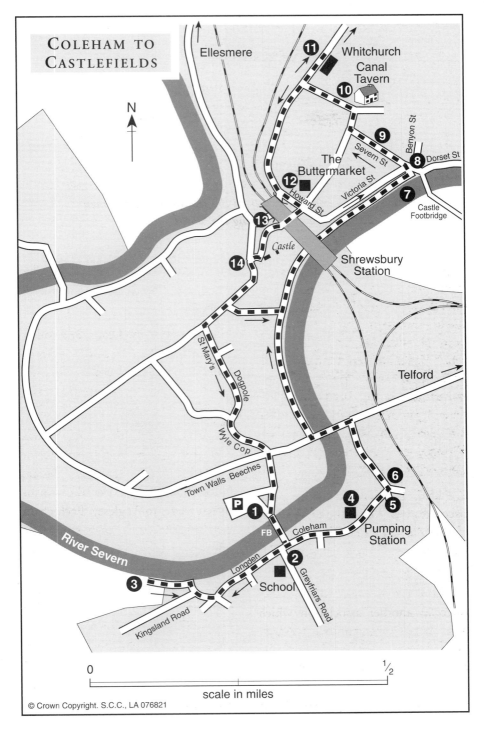

COLEHAM TO CASTLEFIELDS

N

Ellesmere

Whitchurch

Canal Tavern

Benyon St

Severn St

The Buttermarket

Dorset St

Victoria St

Howard St

Castle Footbridge

Castle

Shrewsbury Station

St Mary's

Dogpole

Telford

Wyle Cop

Town Walls Beeches

P

FB

Coleham

Pumping Station

River Severn

Longden

Greyfriars Road

School

Kingsland Road

0   ½

scale in miles

© Crown Copyright. S.C.C., LA 076821

11

employed in a series of great works. He made bridges from Scotland to Plymouth and even for Sweden. He had foundries, ironworks, timber-yards, brick-yards, coal-wharfs and limeworks (see also Llanymynech walk). Greyfriars Bridge, on which you stand, was made in Dudley. You will by now have noticed it is a hog-backed Pratt truss, or lattice girder, bridge.

2 Turn right along the high street, Longden Coleham, towards the buildings with the tall chimney. Pass Rowland's fruit and vegetable business housed there and take Kingsland Road to the right. Follow the public footpath signposted down to the river on your right.

Facing you is Burr's Field and Recreation Ground, a green souvenir of a 19th century red lead works. Thomas Burr, a plumber who had a business at the bottom of Wyle Cop, bought the factory in 1829. Alderman Charles Bage, who features elsewhere in the story, "was possessed of talent and understanding, but was not a man of business". Although his patented steam looms made a better quality linen in his 'bold' fireproof building, the business was declared bankrupt. So it was sold to Burr. Now clouds of smoke poured from chimneys too low to disperse the "noxious and offensive effluvia". The neighbours were driven out of their houses and even residents high on the

other bank in Belmont or The Crescent could detect a metallic taste in the smoke.

Mr Trouncer, the owner of the brewery whose chimney you have just passed, led the attack. He sent sods of turf from the meadow next to the brewery and from one next to the lead works for analysis. The analyst found 12 grams of red lead in the grass near the works. Strange to relate, on the sale of the land to the lead works for the building of a shot tower, Mr Trouncer ceased to advocate legal proceedings against the polluter.

3. Return to Longden Coleham past the footbridge.

The Council School in Greyfriars Road is well worth a peek en route.

Architect Wendy James' dramatic steel portico is her homage to the suburb's industrial past.

4. Stop when you reach Coleham Pumping Station on your left.

The chapel-like exterior, railings and impressive entrance steps proclaim this is a temple of cleanliness. Inside there are two beam engines, boilers, gleaming tiles and one of Hazeldine's Menai Bridge links. Without its beam engines, the town would have choked on its own filth. (For limited opening times phone 01743 362947).

The social, particularly hygiene, revolution limped along a hundred years or so behind the industrial take-off. The Severn had always been Shrewsbury's most convenient sewer. Indeed, a local act imposed a fine of £5 on "anyone who shall NOT EMPTY ... the soil of his necessary house or privy into the Severn, so that the filth and excrement therefrom be completely and effectually carried away by the stream." By 1850 there were fourteen outlets for raw sewage to the river. But there was still opposition to proposals for improvements to the General Board of Health. There are always some, presumably immune to cholera and dysentery, who cannot abide 'throwing money' at the infrastructure.

Coleham Pumping Station

Shrewsbury began the 20th century with a clean sheet. On New Year's Day 1901 the Mayoress opened Coleham Pumping Station, part of a scheme for new sewers and a sewage farm at Monkmoor.

5. Continue along Longdon Coleham to the flats on your left.

What high hopes are buried beneath these flats. "Immense wealth seemed to offer itself to all speculations, of the nature of that which gave birth to the Coleham Manufactory". It began in 1790 when a clergyman of great respectability and his brother-in-law sank £20,000 into the Shrewsbury Woollen Manufactory. But they could not stand the heat of the Industrial Revolution, after twelve months they gave up. The two 'immense' five-storey buildings were used to house French prisoners-of-war.

Yet Shrewsbury always seemed right for textile manufacture. Wages were 40% below those in Lancashire. Hand-loom weaving of linen meant skilled hands. The Coleham Cotton Manufactory began production "under the most favourable circumstances". But cheap labour proved a dangerous illusion; the local linen mills had mopped up the available labour. Farm workers found it difficult to adapt to the factory system, and when they were trained, they left for the fleshpots of Manchester or Stockport.

13

The site seemed to be cursed. When the owner, Charles Hulbert, tried property development, "nearly fifty neat dwellings for workmen for which there was a great demand", the Severn deluged the lower houses seven times in two years. A tenant leased part of the factory to make linen. He died unexpectedly. Hulbert gave up the unequal struggle and "left with deep sorrow his Miniature Castle, his little flourishing plantations, affectionate tenants and neighbours." Wool, cotton, and linen had been tried, the straw they had wanted to spin into gold, proved stubborn.

6. Turn left at the T-junction ahead and left again onto the English Bridge. Walk across the river. Then cross over the road and descend some steps leading to the towpath downstream to Castlefields.

The original railway bridge ahead of you between the two steel bridges is by Robert Stephenson and Joseph Locke (1849).

7. Just before you reach the next small footbridge across the river, turn left up a ramp leading into Dorset Street. Turn left again, but pause on the corner of Benyon Street.

Shrewsbury's chequered textile history Part III: Hopes were high that linen would provide the town with a secure source of employment and wealth. Benyon & Bage's Canal Terminus flax mill employed over 400 people. The splendid five storey mill ran almost the entire length of the present Benyon Street, with another long building at 90. The designer of the revolutionary fire-proof iron-framed Ditherington flax mill, Charles Bage, was also a partner in this enterprise.

8. Carry on up Dorset Street and its continuation Severn Street as far as the three-storeyed houses on the right.

This is the only part of the mill to survive. It was probably the weaving shop and warehouse (1810). When the main mill was demolished several former employees continued to make linen cloth here. Inside, the historic pillars and beams designed by Bage and cast by Hazeldine shoot up from the cellars every seven feet or so through the living rooms and bed rooms.

From the walkway at the rear of the building, it is easier to detect this was once a factory. The largest windows on the top floor are original. On the cottage wall at the side you may decipher "Minn & Co Home Made Linen Warehouse". Robert Minn was Benyon's cashier and carried on the business here until the 1850s.

9. Go to the top of Severn Street, turn right for a short distance on Beacall's Lane.

Across the way, The Canal Tavern, a typical boatmen's inn, has been marooned since the last narrowboat, carrying tar to the nearby gasworks ceased working in 1936. The canal bed is immediately behind the pub. It passed under the road and into the terminal basin, now the BR car park.

10. Take Gashouse Lane down to Castle Foregate. Cross over the road and go right a short distance.

Stop when you reach a bricked-up archway for wagons on the opposite side of the road. On the board below the line of the roof you can just discern the words Speed the Plough under the layers of paint. This was Thomas Corbett's Perseverance Ironworks, makers of agricultural machinery. With the decline of Hazeldine's after his death, this was Shrewsbury's biggest foundry employing several hundred men in the second half of the 19th century. The dates on successive additions to the building testify to rapid expansion in the 1870s.

11. Cross over to the Morriss's side of the road and go back towards town. Turn left into Howard Street and stop at the Buttermarket.

The first canal to reach Shrewsbury was a modest 17 mile tub-boat canal linking the town with the East Shropshire coalfield, but still isolated from the national network. Until the canal opened in 1796 heavy coal carriages had been churning up the Holyhead Road making it impassable.

The Buttermarket (1835) marks the time when the Shrewsbury Canal was up-graded to accept 70ft long narrowboats. The town was linked to the West Midlands via the Newport branch of the Birmingham & Liverpool Junction Canal. How the Victorians worshipped their Temples of Commerce. How fitting to drive a wagon through this great Doric portico, unload the goods at the wharf alongside and see them off, for Bristol, Liverpool, Manchester and even London. If you look across the car-park, to the right at the back you will see the sheds which were used to ripen Messrs Fyffes' bananas.

12. Up Howard Street and take The Dana, the footbridge over the tracks. Pause when you have a good view of the station.

When the joint station, shared by four separate railway companies, was built in 1848, Shropshire was one of the last counties to receive the railway. The local paper was un-impressed. "Shrewsbury will rue the day when the first snort of the iron-horse was heard at the station."

13. Follow The Dana to Castle Gates and turn left, before turning left again and into the castle grounds.

On your left a 19th century Cabbies' Rest; a shelter from The Square for drivers of Hansom cabs.

Follow the winding path to your right up to the small belvedere, Laura's Tower.

"I am again commanding officer in this renowned fortress" wrote Telford in January 1787. He had been given the job of renovating the derelict Castle by its owner William Pulteney, MP for Shrewsbury. Shropshire was Telford's springboard, what splendid paradox that the career of our greatest Victorian engineer began on the steps of this playful building.

From the steps or the terrace below is a panorama of railway lines. The station juts out over the river. Across the river to the left are the lines to Birmingham and London. To the right lines to Hereford and Worcester. Sandwiched between is Europe's largest manual signalbox, a three-storey listed building, requiring two men to operate its 120 levers.

Beyond the station back along the mainroad going North you can just see against a massive concrete structure, the wrought iron work which tops a wooden tower added to the Ditherington Flax Mill. When Shrewsbury's textile tale was finally spun in 1886 it became a Maltings. The world's first skyscraper with Hazeldine's beams and columns still survives, but awaits a fitting new purpose.

14. You return to the car park either along the river by taking Water Lane to the left from Castle Street or, through town via Castle Street, St Mary's Street, Dogpole and Wyle Cop.

'Merlin' Hazeldine lived at Dogpole House on Dogpole. When he died, aged 77, his famous works were making several pairs of iron lockgates "the largest ever executed". Busts of Hazeldine and John Simpson (see Chirk Walk) by Chantrey are in St Chad's Church.

Laura's Tower

16

BRIDGNORTH

OS. Map 1:50,000 sheet 138, starting point GR:719 928

Distance - 3 miles

In the 17th century the Severn was Europe's second busiest river and Bridgnorth was Shropshire's busiest port. It was the Severn which stimulated and sustained the Industrial Revolution which erupted on its banks. The walk begins on the site of one of Bridgnorth's three dockyards and takes you to the lodgings and watering holes of the port's Bargemen and sailors. It also charts the rise of steam locomotion, which would eventually kill off river transport. You will see the birthplace of the world's first passenger locomotive, Britain's last surviving inland cliff railway and one of its finest surviving steam railways - the Severn Valley Railway.

1. Parking - Take the road from Low Town in the direction of Kidderminster (A442). Turn right down Severn Street and park on the river bank opposite the island.

Two hundred years ago the river would have been all of a flutter with the sails of trows and single masted barges or frigates, many of which were built on this bank, in one of Bridgnorth's three dockyards. Other boats were docked on the metal rings, which are still attached to the bridge. Men unloaded barges of coal from the Gorge or wine from Bristol, and clothes and fishing nets hung out to dry on the banks. In the mid-eighteenth century there were 75 vessels operating from Bridgnorth, 214 operating between here and Coalbrookdale. The Severn was not only an invaluable means of import-

ing raw materials and exporting product: it also transported the Darby family, their contemporaries and their customers. Early one morning in 1750 a midshipman left Shrewsbury in a passenger wherry. He breakfasted in Bridgnorth, had tea in Bewdley and arrived in Worcester for 9 o'clock.

The midshipman was lucky - for long periods of the year the water was too low to navigate and bargemen would have to wait for sudden increases in water level called "flushes".

2. Climb up the iron-rimmed steps onto the bridge.

As a port, Bridgnorth attracted industry, including iron. The clock tower in front of you is a memorial to the world's first passenger steam locomotive, built here, in John

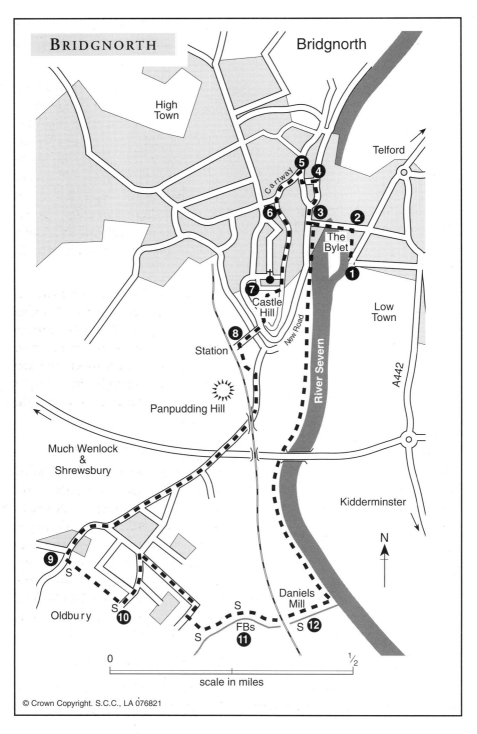

Hazeldine's Iron Foundry. In 1808, Richard Trevithick took his locomotive "Catch Me who Can" to London, hoping to draw investors. A circular track was laid near Euston where it cost a shilling to number among the world's first steam-drawn passengers. Unfortunately "Catch Me Who Can" failed to attract commercial interest. A model of a Trevithick steam engine can be seen in the North Gate museum, High Town.

Cross the bridge, noticing Ridleys "The Oldest Firm of Seedsmen in Great Britain".

With side door and hoist, the building is a typical quayside warehouse.

Most vessels on the Severn were clinker-built - from over-lapping planks - with masts that could be lowered to pass under bridges. To continue up river, a towing rope was thrown from the bridge onto the boat, and the vessel hauled through the arch. Grooves made by ropes are still visible under the arches.

3. Turn right along the road following the river.

Boats were hauled along the Severn by men known as bow-haulers. There were between four and eight men pulling each craft on ropes looped over their chests and shoulders. Thomas Telford decried the work as "barbarous and slavish". Richard Reynolds, one of the Coalbrookdale ironmasters, described it as "destructive of the morals of the people engaged in it".

In 1771 an Act of Parliament approved the building of a horse tow-path from Coalbrookdale to Bewdley. There was an outcry from riverside people and bow-haulers, who feared the loss of their livelihood. It was not until twenty-six years later that Shropshire ship-owners, iron-masters and coal-owners subscribed £5,000. Work on the towpath finally began in 1799.

The road on which you are standing, was built during a harsh Victorian winter, as part of a job creation scheme. It floats on sugar bags weighed down with rocks. You can still see the wrought iron staples holding the blocks of stone on the quayside.

4. Turn left up Bank Steps.

These steps were used by donkeys fetching and carrying goods to the quay. They were laden with wicker "kypes" or panniers. Going down you would find Shropshire produce varying from manure to cheese, from lead to stockings, silk and lace. Coming up the kypes might be filled with wine, spices and brandy from Bristol, or coal from Broseley.

Turn right into Friar Street.

Looking toward the river, and to your left down the valley, you can see a gothic sandstone house, Fort Pendlestone, where the road to Telford nears the Severn. In 1760 Abraham Darby II leased Pendlestone to smelt iron. It later became a spinning mill for rug and carpet making, the principal industry in nineteenth century Bridgnorth. Victoria's Diamond Jubilee throne, stood upon a carpet made here in Bridgnorth.

Walk to The Cartway.

The Cartway was the route taken by carts and wagons to the port. The sturdy shutters are designed to protect windows from the six to eight jostling horses needed to pull a stagecoach or loaded wagon. Just to your left the cafe on the corner was once the Magpie. Like the Blackboy further up the Cartway, this was one of the pubs frequented by the workers off the barges, trows and dockyards. Some lodged here in the Cartway and were entertained by local girls. Others slept on the cargo or under awnings on the barges.

The large timber-framed house on your right was built for a barge-owner, Richard Forester (or Foster) in 1580. The main concentration of Severn barge-owners and crews was here in Bridgnorth and in the Gorge. Two doors below the Wesleyan Chapel, was home to the last man who worked donkeys between High and Low-town. He stabled them in the back and they emerged onto the Cartway via his living room.

5. Walk up the Cartway. As the road levels out turn left along the footpath sign-posted "Cliff Valley Railway".

During the eighteenth and nineteenth centuries, while Low Town was a thriving port with all the accompanying vigour and vice, High Town was becoming a popular resort with the wealthy but unlanded classes. At the end of the century the Bridgnorth Castle Hill Railway Company was formed with the aim of conveying visitors and residents between the two towns whilst avoiding the obvious disadvantages of the Cartway.

The result was the shortest and steepest inland railway in the country. The Rose and Crown pub, which stood at the bottom of the incline, was replaced by the Lower Station, Temperance Restaurant and Refreshment House. The railway was operated hydraulically. A tank on the car at the top of the incline was filled with water until the car was heavy enough to glide downhill and raise the car at the bottom. The full car was emptied at the bottom and the process repeated. Today the railway is operated electrically. It is the ONLY inland cliff railway remaining in Britain and operates a continuous service daily.

6. Continue along Castle Walk, which proffers, according to King Charles I, the finest views in the kingdom. Turn right toward the church.

St Mary's was designed by Thomas Telford. Telford trained as an architect but decided to devote the greater part of his life to the "more important" opportunities afforded by the industrial revolution. Nonetheless his distinctive architectural style can be spotted all over the county. Behind, in the churchyard, is the grave-slab for the Hazeldines, one of the great iron dynasties. Like many fashionable graves at the time, it is forged of the metal on which they built their fortune.

Cliff Railway

7. **Head left, noticing the famous Leaning Tower of Bridgnorth, perfectly balanced at an angle three times that of its Italian counterpart. Head for the barley sugar iron bandstand, and continue straight on to the far right-hand corner of the castle grounds. Climb down Cannon Steps to the busy New Road. Cross the road and go over the footbridge to the Severn Valley Railway.**

In 1808 Trevithick and Rastrick's steam locomotive failed to attract any investors. By 1830 Britain had caught Railway Mania. Plans for a line to run from Shrewsbury to Hartlebury were laid - and abandoned. Twenty years later they were revived by the Severn Valley Railway. The line was to be worked by the Oxford, Worcester and Wolverhampton Company - O.W.& W. Locals, who had witnessed thirty years of delays, renamed the company "Oh! Worse and Worse". The line opened in 1862 and blew the final whistle on river trade. All major East Shropshire industries had their own sidings off the branch lines. Ten years later there were only five barge owners remaining in the Gorge.

It would be more than a hundred years, however, before the line brought the prosperity its supporters had imagined. In the nineteenth century Bridgnorth ceased to be an industrial centre of any importance. In 1965 the railway closed and the Preservation Society was formed. Despite opposition from the County Council, they bought the line from Bridgnorth to Hampton Loade for £25,000. From a Victorian pub on the station to drivers making tea on the engine, it provides an all encompassing experience of the heady days of steam. It attracts thousands of visitors each year and is regarded as the most picturesque steam railway in Britain.

8. For a short route return over the footbridge and turn right on the busy New Road back to the bridge (no.3).

To continue the walk to the SVR viaduct, working flour mill and riverpath - go left from the foot-bridge, down a flight of steps to the Oldbury Road opposite a garage. Go right following the Oldbury Road to the fork. At the fork go right.

Continue for half a mile. Just beyond the village of Oldbury, past the turning for Manor Farm, you will see a way-marked footpath on your left.

9. Cross the stile. Walk down the left hand side of the field to a former field boundary marked by a row of trees. Cross the stile on your left.

10. Follow the track straight on to a T-junction. Go right down another track. Just after the track veers sharply right there is a way-marked footpath on the left. Follow the footpath through a tunnel of hawthorn to a stile. Cross the stile. Cross the sloping field diagonally to a stile in the far left corner.

11. Follow the path over several footbridges to a fork in the path. Bear right at the fork heading for the railway viaduct. The footpath dives under the fourth arch. Cross the stile to Daniel's Mill.

This is the largest waterwheel powering a cornmill in Britain. The tributaries along this stretch of the Severn were also used to power paper mills and iron forges. Daniel's Mill has been in the same family and remains virtually unaltered since the eighteenth century.

12. Walk down the drive to the road. Cross the road. A little way to your left is a rusty farm-gate leading to the river path. Go through the gate

and follow the river into town to the quay by the bridge.

By the end of the nineteenth century coal, pig iron and limestone were no longer carried on the Severn. The only significant freight was bricks and roofing tiles from Jackfield. On a January afternoon in 1895 a barge carrying firebricks ran into the bridge and sank: a dramatic finale to the commercial navigation of the Shropshire Severn.

Cross the bridge to return to your car.

Daniel's Mill

CHIRK

OS Map 1:50,000 Sheet No. 126, Starting point GR: 285 378

Distance: 3 miles (If you intend going through, rather than over, Chirk Tunnel, it is advisable to take a torch).

Three miles that tell us more about the transport revolution than anywhere else. Not just the breathtaking monuments, but the triumphs over 'It can't be done' and the tragedies of the even more grandiose failures.

It is literally a cross-roads of Telford's career. With his 'stream in the sky' Telford sent his reputation soaring. He transformed a maze of old roads in a muddy morass into the finest road in Europe. The first Shropshire passenger train ran through here. But there might have been much more. A canal to link Bristol and Liverpool and the main railway line to Ireland. There is ample compensation, the prettiest wrought iron gates in the kingdom and the story of a unique horse-drawn tramway.

1. Take the brown-signposted road from the town towards Chirk Castle and park on a straight stretch near the railway station. Follow the road away from town towards the castle gates.

Known locally as the 'pretty gates', they were made in the early 18th century by the Davies Brothers, blacksmiths from Croes Foel, just south of Bersham near Wrexham. Suns, animals, tendrils in black and gold make the gates and wings among the most ornate in the country.

2. Take the path, signposted with the Red Hand, to the left of the castle park. Go through to the side of the double gates. Keep straight ahead until you come to the signposts, either left, for those with pushchairs, or right, a steeper descent through the wood, to the B4500. Cross the road and turn right to the bottom of the hill.

3. Just before the bridge, cross the stile or go through the gate into the field beside the river.

Pont Faen is an attractive stone bridge well over three hundred years old.

4. Follow the footpath beside the river downstream towards the viaduct and aqueduct.

If a 100ft high twelve arch viaduct seems a little grand for the line between two county towns, it could have been a key link in a scheme to

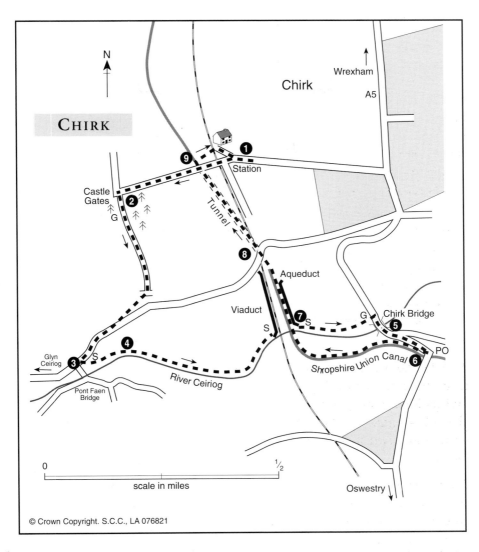

create a rival ferry port to Holyhead at Porth Dynlleyn. Railway Mania possessed the 1840s speculators much as the property bubble did their successors in the 1980s. But the reality of expensive engineering and grey Welsh mountains destroyed the scheme's 'painted delusions, gaudy shams, gilded puffs and painted paragraphs' derided by a Shrewsbury paper. This magnificent 846ft long monument was designed by Henry Robertson, engineer to the Shrewsbury & Chester Railway and built by Thomas Brassey, the greatest railway contractor.

4. Cross the two stiles under the

25

viaduct and aqueduct and follow the river until you reach the stone bridge and Telford's A5. Take the ramp to the left of the bridge, climb over the stile and turn right over the bridge.

Chirk Bridge

Thomas Telford designed the bridge, one of forty road bridges for which he was responsible between 1790 and 1796 as Surveyor of Public Works for Shropshire. It was built in 1793 by John Simpson of Shrewsbury. When the bridge was widened with reinforced concrete in 1926 the original masonry was retained. Looking over the parapet on the Shropshire side, you can see where breakwaters were added in 1844, to prevent the Ceiriog from undermining the abutments.

From the departure of the Romans until the M1 in 1957, this was the only major road scheme to be paid for by central government. The new Irish MPs insisted on an improved link between Dublin and Westminster. London mail coaches could not travel beyond Shrewsbury. The further west you travelled, the worse the roads became. It took fifteen years to complete. Telford, who had earned the nickname 'the Colossus of Roads', boasted it would last for centuries. He adopted the Roman idea of carefully graded stones. The poet Southey, friend of Telford, wrote "This road is as near perfect as possible. After the foundation has been laid, the workmen are charged to throw out every stone which is bigger than a hen's egg. Every precaution is taken to render the work permanent in all its parts." Iron tyres broke tiny fragments off the top layer of stones and, packing the grit down between the stones, created a smooth, almost water-tight surface.

The roads to Holyhead from Shrewsbury and Chester are the only significant examples in England of Telford's technique. Elsewhere the trusts preferred Macadam's cheaper, more cheerful solution.

5. Bear right past the Bridge Inn up the minor road signposted Weston Rhyn. The sub post office, with its Welsh postal address, is the only

'Welsh' post office in England. It sells a good range of postcards and local books.

Look at the underside of Bridge 21 the iron supporting ribs are somewhat unusual. To your left, about half a mile away at Gledrid, was the original terminus of the horse-drawn Glyn Valley Tramway, where slate and granite were shipped by canal.

6. Take the canal towpath to the right towards Chirk.

No.3 Aqueduct Cottages has a number of forbidding cast-iron signs and other canaliana. "This path on sufferance only" "NO person is allowed to pass over the aqueduct with their bicycle. July 1918".

7. Walk on to the aqueduct.

This aqueduct has some stories to tell. Of Canal Mania, when in the rush to subscribe for shares, speculators slept two or three to a bed, and six even arrived in a funeral coach. 10th September 1792 about noon the books of the Ellesmere Canal Navigation opened, "ere sun set near a million pounds was confided to the care of the company".

Would they have slept easy had they known that the scheme to link the Mersey, Dee and Severn, for tapping the minerals of North Wales and Shropshire depended on an incredible two and a half mile great tunnel near Ruabon? That Thomas Telford had no previous experience of building canals? Better perhaps to have stayed in their own bed and kept the money in the mattress.

Chirk Aqueduct

Encouragingly, Telford came with the recommendation of the Coalbrookdale ironmasters. Faced by the challenge of crossing the Ceiriog here at Chirk and the Dee at Pontcysyllte, he created his "stream in the sky", a revolutionary weight-saving iron aqueduct. Because of the enormous load of water, clay bed and stone, previous canals had to cross a valley at low level on squat brick arches. Time-consuming and expensive locks were needed on both sides of the valley.

The foundation stone of the 200ft. aqueduct was laid on 17th June 1796. It was completed in 1801 by a team whose "combined skill was unrivalled in England", according to LTC Rolt, Telford's biographer. John Simpson (builder of the bridge over the Ceiriog), William Hazeldine, called 'Merlin' by Telford (see Shrewsbury Walk) who made the iron bed plates, and John Wilson, who used a new hollow wall technique to reduce the weight of the piers and spandrels.

The over-ambitious canal never came near completion. To the north no alternative was found to the great tunnel and to the south work was abandoned a few miles from Shrewsbury at Weston Lullingfields. A landlocked canal had been created. To avoid disaster, the company was forced to employ a roundabout route via the Chester Canal.

The significance of Chirk is not, therefore, the canal itself, but as the cross roads of Telford's career. Before this canal he was an architect. Here he laid the foundation of an international reputation as an engineer. It is extraordinary that at Chirk we have a canal and a road, an aqueduct and bridge by the greatest engineer of Victorian Britain.

Chirk Tunnel was built solely to avoid intrusion on the Castle estate.

8. Walkers who dislike dark, confined spaces should take the path to the right of the tunnel up to the road and turn left along the pavement. Soon after the de-restriction sign, on the right you will see a kind of kissing gate of scaffolding poles and the sign in Welsh 'Llwybr Cyhoeddus' - public footpath - take this through the wood and field until you come out on the road to the castle gates where you began.

Adventurous moles who take the tunnel, can reflect on how much worse it must have been when boatmen 'legged' their boats through. The towpath is another Telford innovation, the first to be built in a tunnel.

9. After a quarter of a mile you emerge with some relief in the cutting on the far side. In twenty or thirty yards is a sloping path back to your right leading to the road. Turn left along the road to the railway bridge.

On your left, under Canal Wood Industrial Estate was the terminus of the unique Glyn Valley Tramway. It was one of the few examples in this country of a narrow gauge railway running beside a road the B4500 to Glyn Ceiriog. Slate for the booming towns and later granite setts for the new street tramways in the cities were carried in mixed trains with passengers to the main-line GWR station. Round trips from Llangollen were an early tourist attraction. Down the canal by horse-drawn boat to Chirk, the Glyn Valley Tramway to Glyn Ceiriog and 3½ miles on foot back over the hill to Llangollen.

On the main-line there were bands, banquets and bells for the first railway passenger service to reach Shropshire. On October 12th 1848 a thousand passengers made the inaugural journey from Shrewsbury to Chester. They had a cheerless coming of it in Chester, however, 'neither a biscuit to eat, nor a glass with which one brother corporator could hob nob with another'. Whether in search of biscuits or the odd glass or two, when the train departed for Shrewsbury, a hundred Salopians were left behind. Even those on the train were two hours late back in Shrewsbury. The Railway Age had arrived.

Return to your car.

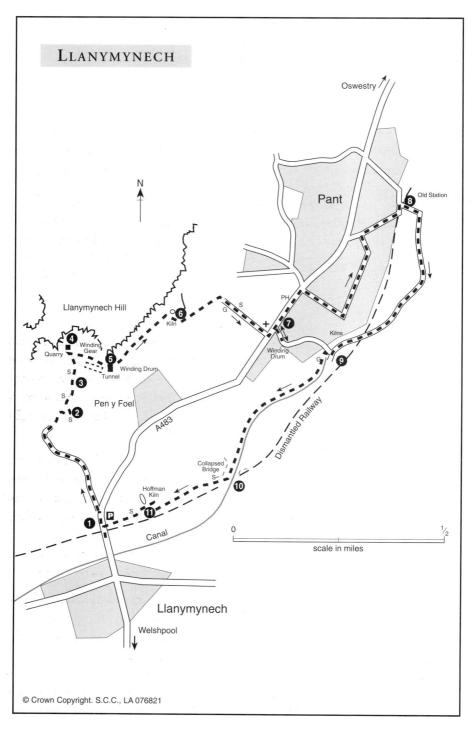

LLANYMYNECH

Oswestry

N

Pant

Old Station ❽

Llanymynech Hill

❻
Kiln

S
G

PH

❼

❹
Winding Gear
Quarry

❺

Winding Drum

Tunnel

Kilns

❾

Winding Drum

G

❸
S

S

Pen y Foel

A483

Dismantled Railway

❷
S

Collapsed Bridge
S

❿

Hoffman Kiln

❶
P
S

⓫

Canal

0   ½
scale in miles

Llanymynech

Welshpool

LLANYMYNECH

OS Map 1:50,000 Sheet 126, Starting point GR: 266 213

Distance: 3 miles

Llanymynech Hill has delivered up human skeletons, Roman tools,
battleaxes and a hoard of silver denarii discovered by local schoolboys.
It was here Charles Darwin first put his hand to the study of field geology:
"Carboniferous limestone" he wrote in his notebook.
The same limestone was to prove Llanymynech's real treasure.
It was used as flux to keep the iron flowing in the East Shropshire blast
furnaces. It fertilised the land, freeing a labour force to work in the cities
and helped re-house them as lime mortar and plaster. In mid-nineteenth
century Shropshire, limestone was in short supply. For Llanymynech,
and the neighbouring village of Pant, it was boom time.

A gentle yet dramatic walk to the vast quarries on Llanymynech Hill, now reserved for swifts, kestrels and wild orchids. Along the network of disused tramways, canals and railways, the walk returns via the former limeworks to the revolutionary Hoffman Kiln a rare gem of industrial engineering.

Park on the Heritage Area car park, just north of Llanymynech village.

The sudden change in Llanymynech's fortunes is reflected in its architecture. The high street is dominated by large Victorian hotels, houses and pubs.

Walk up to the main road. Go right and take the first left in the direction of Pen y Foel. Follow the signs for Offa's Dyke Footpath. They will lead you up the lane until it veers sharply left. Take the lane to your right. It climbs steeply, passes several cottages then comes to a dead-end. Cross the stile straight ahead of you.

2. The path leads uphill through the woodland. Cross a second stile. Follow the path until you see an arrow pointing straight up the hill. Climb this steep path to a T-junction and cross a stile on your left. Walk a few paces to a fork.

Between the two paths ahead of you, in the bushes, are the remains of a winding drum. If you look on the ground to your right you will see a stone grooved by the ropes used to lower wagons of limestone down the incline to the transport systems and kilns below.

3. Go right into the quarry. Keep to the right-hand face until you reach an explosives store cut into the rock.

In 1692 the first ever use of gunpowder in underground blasting took place on Llanymynech Hill. The extensive use of explosives in limestone extraction made working the rock extremely dangerous. In 1858 the death of a rockman in a blasting accident merited only a couple of column inches on page 3 of the Oswestry Advertiser. Robert Morris bored a hole in the rockface and, as usual, packed it with explosives. A spark dropped on the powder before he could stand clear. A later editorial comments "Llanymynech Hill is little better than a huge pitfall and could hardly have been more ingeniously devised, of set purpose, to occasion accidents."

4. From the explosives store head for the winding drum indicated on the map just to the right of the quarry centre.

This winding drum lies at the head of another incline which goes straight through the tunnel in the quarry face. The loaded trucks were assembled on the level ground in front of the winding gear. They were attached to a cable which led round the drum and down the incline where it was hooked onto empty trucks. The loaded trucks passed on rails down the incline and in turn lifted up empty trucks. A brakeman would watch the trucks from the top of the incline and control their rate of descent via a remote-control brake.

Walk down the incline to the tunnel mouth.

Loaded trucks passed through this tunnel, then were pulled by horses or shunted to a second incline lowering them off the hill. Sections of the metal tracks that brought the limestone from this lower quarry face can still be seen on the quarry bed.

5. Return up the incline and walk back to the quarry mouth. At the entrance to the quarry, take the path to the left. It passes the other end of the tunnel and a third set of winding gear on your right. The steel friction strap used to slow down the descending trucks is still attached to the timber. Keep to the broad tramway track.

The quarry's vastness gives some idea of the scale of the industry. By 1855 60,000 tons were being extracted annually. A local historian estimated the combined outputs of nearby Porth-y-Waen and Llanymynech as "70,000 tonnes of burnt lime, thus showing the extended use now made of limestone in the cultivation of farmlands". Equally the blast furnaces of the iron industry were hungry for flux, and vast blocks were needed in building and engineering.

6. Just before the main path swings left, you will see a barbed wire fence straight ahead of you. Look over the fence to see a tree growing out of a lime kiln. Follow the path until you reach a farm gate. To the left of the gate you will see a stile. Cross the stile and follow the path (another former tramway) straight on. Go through two kissing gates, pass the Methodist church and cross the main road. Walk down the track opposite to a restored winding drum.

The drum has been re-equipped with brake, chains and even the limestone in the truck. The limestone went from here down the overgrown incline to a bank of kilns on the canal wharf.

7. Go back to the main road and turn right. Take the road on your right, opposite the Cross Guns. Take the first left and then go right down Smelthouse Lane. At the bottom of the lane you will reach a stone bridge.

In 1796 the Ellesmere Canal stretched out its arm to Llanymynech. Limestone was carried to the industrial market in the north and to agriculture on the Welsh borders. In 1835 a canal wharf at Wappenshall created a better link to Shrewsbury and the blast furnaces of Coalbrookdale. The timing was perfect for Llanymynech as supplies of limestone in East Shropshire were running short.

In 1860 the Oswestry-Newtown railway linked Pant to Aberystwyth, Birmingham, Manchester and London. Behind you stood the platform, tramway, sidings and double-track railway. The railway was also designed to carry limestone from Crickheath Hill Quarries. This arrived in Pant on the tramway and passed through the miniature arch under the canal bridge.

8. Walk over the bridge and turn right down the lane. Follow the lane until you reach a second canal bridge and a bank of five limekilns on your right. Go over the bridge and cross a stile on your right leading to the kilns.

A restored winding drum

Another incline ran from the restored winding drum to this bank of vertical kilns. It is known as Rhiw Revel after the haulage ponies stabled here. Coal was brought along the canal, (now filled in as far as the bridge) and unloaded at the base of the kilns. They were stoked with coal and the limestone was added from above. The fire was lit and over a period of two or three days the limestone broke down into white calcium oxide, or quick-lime, and carbon dioxide.

Ironically, though the water-ways brought the lime-rush to Llanymynech, they could not export quicklime, limestone's most valuable product. When mixed with water quicklime forms slaked lime - the essential component of mortar. Unfortunately the combination also produces heat - enough to destroy the wooden boats which were to ship it to the market. Over a hundred lime kilns had to be built along the length of the Ellesmere Canal. Unprocessed

limestone was transported to the kilns and converted to quicklime in situ before being carted off by local farmers or industry.

9. Return over the bridge and walk down to the canal tow-path. Continue past the abutments of a former railway bridge to a grassed-over pipe crossing the canal. Walk over the canal and up the steps onto the collapsed bridge.

The Shrewsbury-Chester line was eager to benefit from as much of the local mineral traffic as possible. They opened a branch from Llynclys to Porthywaen quarries, to the coalmines near Trefonen and Sweeney Mountain and a siding from a junction just south of Pant into the main kiln site at Llanymynech. The line opened in 1863, crossing the canal at this point, heading up to the kiln site and continuing under the main street. Three years later a second railway was laid from

The bank of five limekilns

34

Shrewsbury to Llanymynech. With typical Victorian confidence, the line was intended to create a link from the Potteries to the Welsh coast, but never grew beyond a precarious local service. Nevertheless the volatile quicklime could now be processed on site and transported for a fraction of the cost. New, larger kilns were required to process lime here in Llanymynech.

10. Go left to a stile leading into a field. Keep to the left of the field heading for a chimney towering above the trees. Cross a second stile at the far end of the field. Walk up the steps to the vast chimney of the revolutionary Hoffman kiln. Step inside the kiln and marvel at the cloister-like arches and chambers, still coated with a white icing of lime.

The Hoffman, or ring kiln was heralded as the most efficient of all time. It produced a purer lime and used less fuel than vertical kilns. The kiln worked continuously and had to be manned day and night. A fire would pass at a rate of two to four feet per hour, from one chamber on to its neighbour continuously circling the fourteen arches. At all times one chamber would be empty, one charging, and the rest either pre-heating, cooling or under fire. The height of the chimney was essential to produce a powerful draught. The work was highly skilled. Scorched hands and feet, lime burns, intense heat and sulphur fumes contributed to what was described as "working in the jaws of Hell".

Throughout the nineteenth century the limestone industry flourished. The Hoffman kiln was built around 1880. But chemical fertilisers replaced lime and the Shropshire Iron Age was over.

The kiln could not combat a dwindling market and it closed on the day the First World War broke out. Miraculously it has survived for over one hundred years. In 1995 it was restored as a memorial to Llanymynech's century in the lime-light.

11. Come back down the steps. Turn right on the main path passing a huge vertical kiln on your right. When you reach a red-brick building, the former stable block, go left to return through the Heritage Area, over a stile, to the car-park.

The Lilleshall walk in David Gregory's 'Walks Around Telford' explores some even older lime kilns and a remarkable transport system - the first canal to be built in Shropshire.

SNAILBEACH

OS Map 1:50,000 Sheet No 126, Starting point GR:373 023
Distance 4 miles

*When lead was almost as valuable as gold, this was the Klondyke.
In the 18th and 19th centuries Britain was the world's leading producer.
Snailbeach was the richest mine per acre in Europe. It produced 167,000 tons
of ore, worth around £50 million at today's prices. 500 workers, a dozen
steam engines, its own railway and underground, the cacophony of blasting,
rock drills, hammers and rumbling wagons extracting up to 3,000 tons of
ore annually. Lead to shoot you dead, lead for your coffin, for roofing
and plumbing, paint, enamelling, lead-acid batteries, ringing lead
crystal glasses and pottery glazes, even for whitening bread.*

1. Park in the car park by Snailbeach village hall. Cross the road, go through the kissing gate and start up the hill.

On your left, before reclamation, was the White Tip, the great Snailbeach landmark. $2^1/_2$ million tons of waste from the crushing mill and from below ground. The whiteness was due to barytes and calcite quartz in the waste. From 1900 a Halvans (Cornish for waste) Company recovered spar from the White Tip. The quartz and calcite chips were used for pebble-dashing houses.

The mineral sorting floors, where the spoil was processed, and the remains of the Halvans Engine House are on the left of the path.

*Halvans Engine House
- illustrated as it was
in 1964. 'Halvans' is a Cornish
mining term for mine waste.*

36

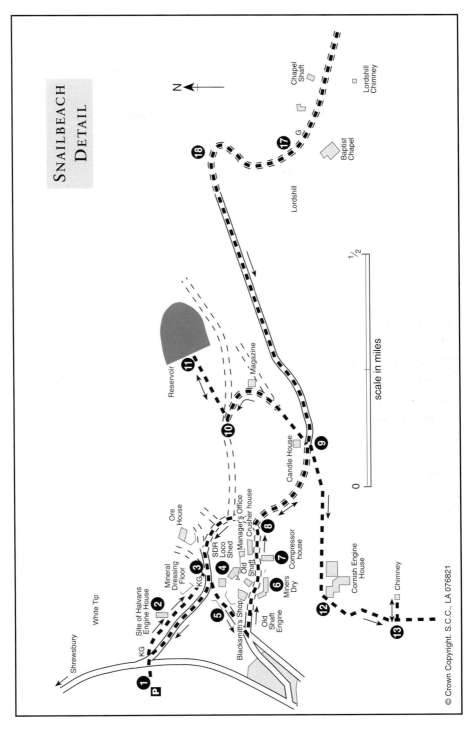

SNAILBEACH DETAIL

Shrewsbury

White Tip

Site of Halvans
Engine House

Ore House

Mineral Dressing Floor

Reservoir

Magazine

SDR Loco Shed

Old Shaft

Manager's Office

Crusher house

Candle House

Blacksmith's Shop

Compressor house

Miners Dry

Old Shaft Engine

Cornish Engine House

Chimney

Lordshill

Chapel Shaft

Lordshill Chimney

Baptist Chapel

G

N

0   ½

scale in miles

37

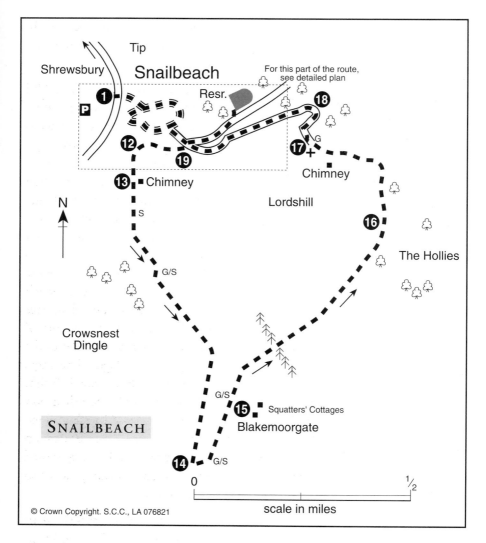

Shrewsbury

Tip

Snailbeach

For this part of the route, see detailed plan

P

1

Resr.

18

12

19

17 G +

Chimney

13 Chimney

S

N

16

Lordshill

The Hollies

Crowsnest Dingle

G/S

S NAILBEACH

G/S

15 Squatters' Cottages

Blakemoorgate

14 G/S

0   1/2

© Crown Copyright. S.C.C., LA 076821

scale in miles

---

2. Continue up the hill to the Stone Bank.

This is a drop in what was the ocean of the White Tip.

Lead may have been as good as gold, but it was never easy to win from the earth. Before the molten metal crystallised into lead ore it was forced into the fissures of the rocks from below. Typically, the veins at Snailbeach are almost vertical ribbons of lead ore in the quartzite. Following the ribbons of lead into the earth, the mine eventually reached a depth of 2250ft, well below sea-level.

3. Leave by the Kissing Gate. Cross the road.

The infrastructure and buildings you see today on this extraordinary site are the fruits of massive capital investment undertaken in the 1870s and 80s. Ironically, after nearly a hundred years in which Snailbeach had been the most profitable lead mine in England, the end was nigh.

4 Bear right along the railway line

The side-by-side double building is the locomotive shed, for two engines, of the Snailbeach District Railway, opened in 1877. The mining company was a major shareholder in the line, which ran to Minsterley. The Snailbeach site was heavily dependent on coal for the 'Cornish' engines to pump the mine, raise the lead ore, operate the cages for the miners and to drive the machinery - including the lead smelter, there were a dozen places where tons of coal were consumed. The railway cut the cost of bringing coal, and timber, from the Minsterley mine and of shipping out lead and barytes. With just half the standard gauge, 2ft 4ins, the SDR was an economical solution.

5. Follow the line round to the right, between the abutments of a demolished bridge. Take the first turn to the left up the slope, as far as, on your left:

The Blacksmith's Shop; through the window you can see the hearth and a fine pair of forge bellows. The blacksmith's shop would have looked after the machinery on the site, in particular the sharpening of the rock drills.

Behind and to your left is The Old Shaft. Originally this was a ladder shaft. The miners went down a series of ladders to reach the workings, which were 600 feet deep in 1800. When, however, the mine had reached 1500 feet, up to $1^1/_2$ hours were wasted getting to and from the face. In 1872 a horizontal steam engine for winding cages was installed. Wooden headgear over the shaft supported pulleys, one of which you can see nearby. The shaft was widened and deepened. Lengths of timber were bolted to the sides of the shaft to guide the cages. The cages held seven men. From the 750 foot level the miners still made their way to the rest of the workings by ladder. Each day there were 30 to 40 trips up and down. Barytes, a heavy spar used in paper and paint making, was also raised via this shaft.

On the 6th of March 1895 the shaft was the scene of a fatal accident. Seven miners were killed when the steel-wire winding rope broke half way down the shaft. The 7ft 6in high cage was compressed to 18in by the impact, although it is said the watch of one of the miners was still ticking. "Accidental death," returned the jury "caused by the breakage of a defective rope...not properly looked after, and has been used too long." It had been in continuous use for eight years. The cage on display has a short set of rails to enable wagons to be pushed in.

6. Return to the track. On the other side of the track is a group of buildings.

The building on the right was the Old Shaft Engine House. The two-storey building next to it is the Miner's 'Dry' or changing house and barracks, dating from 1872-75.

In the side of the hill on the left of the Miner's Dry is a tunnel sealed by a gate. "Day Level" is an adit - a horizontal shaft for transport or drainage. Iron buckets called kibbles, egg-shaped so they could slip more easily through the narrow seams, were hauled up the shaft to this level. Inside the mine the ore was tipped into wagons which were pushed along rails out of the mine here and on to the Crusher House.

7. Continue along the path. On your right is the Compressor House.

Snailbeach was one of the first mines to begin drilling shot holes for blasting with compressed air drills. The compressor house was built in 1881, even ahead of the pace-setting Cornish industry. The immense stone blocks indicate the size and power of

George's Shaft in the early 1970's which replaced the earlier one in 1914.

the engine. On the left of the building is the boiler shed where they raised steam for the compressor. On the right was a large steel tank for storing compressed air. The air was fed underground via iron pipes, where it also powered small winches to pull the kibbles from lower levels to the main tramways.

On the opposite side of the track is the Crusher House. The wagons arrived at the Crusher House via an elevated tramway. Here the lead was separated from the surrounding quartz before despatch to the smelter.

8. Carry on to the end of the track.

Follow the road uphill to the right.

The last stone building on your left is the Candle House. The miners used to wear bowler hats reinforced with resin. A candle was stuck in the brim of the hat.

9. Take the well-defined path down to the left.

On the right of the path is the magazine, where the gunpowder was stored. For safety the building is well away from the main workings. There are double walls to cut down any blast. Bark on the floor reduced the risk of boots striking a spark.

10. Carry on along the path and walk up the slight incline on your right to the 'New' Reservoir.

As Snailbeach grew, an acute shortage of water for the boilers and ore dressing developed. This reservoir, still impressive today, was built in 1872 as part of the major capital investments. Beyond the reservoir were the Upper Works serving Perkin's Level, a horizontal shaft mining lead and barytes in the hill beyond. When you go back down the embankment, the small building to the right is the Valve House.

11. Go back the way you have come to the road. Cross over and take the well-defined path opposite going uphill into the wood. Climb up until you reach the 'Cornish' Engine House on the left.

At first Snailbeach had been cheap to work. The first 500ft of the mine could be simply, and cheaply, drained through a horizontal shaft driven in from the valley bottom. There were no pumping costs. But as the mine grew, water flowed in at a higher rate.

A waterwheel was erected. It still was not enough. The new agent, charged with increasing the profits, sent for a Cornish giant. Teams of

The Compressor House

sixteen horses hauled the stones for the giant's castle, the 36ft beam, boilers and the 61ins diameter cylinder: loads of ten tons or more, up the hillside you have just climbed.

On the left of the Engine House is Engine Shaft. At 1400 ft this was the deepest shaft. It was the main haulage and pumping shaft. The engine could pump 24,000 litres (5,200 gallons) per hour. It needed five hours pumping in Summer and seven in Winter to keep the mine dry for a day.

On the far side of the shaft was a horizontal winding engine for hauling the kibbles to Day Level.

On the opposite side of the main path, running diagonally across the hill, you can see the line of an inclined plane from the main works area below. A steam winch, located in the Boiler House, would haul trucks of coal up this incline, to feed the boilers of the steam engine.

12. Walk past the Engine House. There is a viewing platform round to the left. Continue uphill until you see a short path on your left leading to the chimney.

Everything about the 'infrastructure' here is on a vast and expensive scale. The chimney is the culmination of a flue which runs underground for half a mile from the lead smelter. Snailbeach was an unusually integrated concern. Unlike other mines,

it smelted lead on the spot rather than shipping it to works on the Dee. The old smelt mill at Pontesford, which had done much to poison workers, populace and agriculture, had been replaced by a new reverbatory mill around 1861. The long flue and high chimney created a powerful draught for the six hearths. Despite the tall chimney, you can still read in a description of the site in 1972 "the stack rises above the dead trees killed by the poisonous smoke it once shed". The flue passes under the chimney from the left. In the grassy bank, turning downhill, are the curved bricks of the flue.

13. Return to the path and keep on uphill, out of the woods over the stile and on to the heath. Head uphill towards the skyline. Head for a gate and stile close together ahead of you. Through the gate and bear left along the fence uphill for some way. Below you on the right is Crow's Nest Dingle. Only one house survives, but there are remains of several more. When you come to a farm gate and stile, go through, or over, and keep on uphill still following the fence. Finally the fence veers off to the left, keep to the narrow path through the heather.

14. The path intersects with a wider track. Turn left. Ignore the farm gates with waymarks, our path continues a little way downhill and becomes a well-defined track.

Over the stile or farm gate.

On the right are several 'squatters' cottages, some in ruins, but one is well preserved. Landowners were usually happy to collect rent from such a remote wild spot. The miners built these houses out of local stone, grew vegetables, kept a pig, and chickens. Their sheep were allowed to graze on the hillside.

The working week, to the dismay of the mine owners, was five days of eight hour shifts. Women and children worked on the surface crushing and preparing the ore for smelting.

15. Over the stile or through the gate. Go half right, heading for the gap in the conifers. Over the stile or through the farm gate.

Through the copse straight ahead, passing an exclosure, a wired-off area to protect trees from grazing animals, on your right.

These gnarled old holly trees are the remains of an ancient forest which once covered the hillside. Some have fallen and are re-shooting from where they landed. Without protection they would eventually be killed off by grazing.

16. The track veers gently to the left and then downhill. When you come to the waymarked post, go down the left-hand track.

To the left of the track is a Chapel Shaft chimney. On the right is the shaft itself and remains of the engine/boiler house. It was believed the main ore vein continued eastwards from here. The Earl of Tankerville, who owned the mineral rights, insisted on continuous exploration until the shaft was 1000ft deep. But the lead vein was cut off just beyond here by the Stiperstones quartzite. The modest spoil heap on the right of the track is indicative of the restricted scale of operations.

17. Carry on along the track. On the left behind the hedge is Lordshill Baptist Chapel (1833 re-built 1873) from which the shaft took its name. Go through the gate and round to the right of the Chapel.

Abandoned cottage at Blackmoorgate

At the back of the graveyard you will find the headstone of Arthur Wardman aged 27. Of the seven men killed when the rope broke at the Old Shaft, he was particularly unfortunate. Another miner in front of him had forgotten to collect his tools, left for sharpening at the Blacksmith's. He made way for Arthur Wardman, who took his place in the fatal cage.

For a few weeks in 1948 this site was miraculously transformed by the magic of the Movies. The clock was turned back to the late 1800s. David O Selznick, the Hollywood producer, was filming Mary Webb's 'Gone To Earth' with his wife, Jennifer Jones, David Farrar, Sybil Thorndike and a 24 year old George Cole.

With your back to the grave, on your left you will see a small flight of steps leading down to the little brook. Here they built a pool, where Cyril Cusack (the Reverend Edward Marsdon) baptises his new wife Jennifer Jones (Hazel Woodus).

At the end of the film Jennifer Jones, the fox in her arms, comes racing down the hillside towards the Chapel before falling to her death in the mine-workings. A starring role for a Snailbeach lead mine.

Return to the track and turn left. Through the gate. The track begins to climb again. Where it meets the metalled road, go round the bend to the right. In the field on your right is the capped shaft of Lordshill.

18. Follow the bend round to the left and continue down the hill.

19. Walk back towards the Stone Bank, taking the right-hand fork at the bottom of the hill. The building on the right before the cottages was the Ore House.

Now you have walked the site you may find it easier to imagine it as "unsurpassed in the United Kingdom or, as a lead mining district, probably in Europe." Robert Horne 1887. But mining lead was always an 'adventure'. Cheaper supplies from abroad drove down prices. Output was reduced. After a brief revival, the "Cornish" engine was sold and pumping ceased in 1911. The mine flooded to the 350ft level.

Barytes could still be mined above this level and recovered from the White Tip.

In all Snailbeach may have produced 100,000 tons. It was even used as screening for nuclear reactors. But let Shakespeare speak the epitaph of this great mine.

but thou, thou meagre lead,

Which rather threatenest than dost promise aught,

Thy paleness moves me more than eloquence;

And here choose I: joy be the consequence!

JACKFIELD AND COALPORT

OS Map 1:50,000 Sheet No.127, Starting point GR: 687 029

Distance: 3 miles

*Three of the Ironbridge Gorge's original seven wonders and
one modern one: Calcutts, Coalport, the Tar Tunnel and the futuristic
Jackfield Free Bridge.*

*If early visitors thought of the flaming furnaces as the Vesuvius of
Shropshire, then Jackfield is its Pompeii. First Calcutts Ironworks, and later
the bottle kilns of the world's two largest tile-making plants laid down their
smoke, soot and ash on the little town. Finally, in 1952, a large
part was engulfed by the flooding of disused clay workings. Like Pompeii,
Jackfield even has its own historic brothel.*

**Take the B4373 and cross the Severn
by the new Jackfield Bridge.**

Designing a neighbour to the world's
most famous bridge would be hard
enough. Having Thomas Telford as a
predecessor posed a unique challenge.
Instead of a boring, 'safe' solution,

Shropshire County Council has
produced this witty Flash Gordon-
style suspension bridge. Technically it
is an asymmetric, cable-stay design.
The 1908 Free Bridge was the first
big reinforced-concrete bridge built
in this country. A portion has been
preserved on the Jackfield side.

**Follow the road round to the left
and cross the old Severn Valley
Railway line.**

The level crossing gates are said to
be the widest in Britain. On
your right is Calcutts
House, now a
B&B, but once
home to the
owners of the
Ironworks. Right
next to the house

*Jackfield
Bridge*

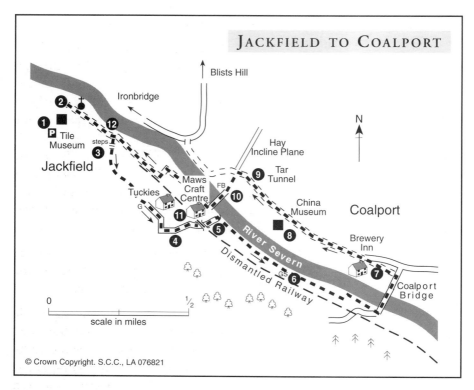

© Crown Copyright. S.C.C., LA 076821

were twenty tar kilns of the British Tar Company. The cannon which defeated Napoleon at Waterloo were made in the foundry and boring mills of Calcutts Ironworks between here and the river.

1. Park at the Jackfield Tile Museum.

The Craven Dunnill factory was built in 1871. With its squat spire and Gothic windows it looks more like a church than a factory - a fitting showroom for the company's products. Chester Cathedral and, nearer to hand, The Tontine Hotel opposite the Iron Bridge, are paved with their decorative tiles.

2. Walk past the front of the factory and turn right. Pass the church on your left. Continue along a 'temporary' (since the 1950s) section of road.

This bank of the Severn Gorge had plentiful deposits of good clay, After centuries of exploitation, the workings literally proved Jackfield's undoing, when a landslip destroyed over fifty houses. Cracks in the factory walls and the flexible road surface are evidence of continued movement.

3. At the fork look for a short flight of steps, leading to a field on the right. The hummocks are signs of

46

clay mining. Work your way across the field to the top left-hand corner. When you come to the top go through a metal gate.

The 'Tuckies' on your left, is the oldest house of any size in the Gorge. Now called Wallace House, it was the home of William Reynolds, an entrepreneur whose astonishing vision kept the Gorge in the van of the Industrial Revolution. More than a most inventive ironmaster, in building the Shropshire Canal, he created the New Town of Coalport. He built an experimental steam-boat and was working on a steam locomotive, when the prototype blew up, killing a workman. With Thomas Telford he worked on the design and manufacture of the world's first cast-iron aqueduct at Longdon-on-Tern.

4. Pass a row of cottages before swinging downhill to the left. Pass under the railway bridge and continue straight ahead, still going downhill. The track passes the beer garden of the Boat Inn, where the level of Severn floods are marked.

5. As the track veers left, take a path leading off to the right, following the riverbank across a field. Before reaching the boundary of the field, walk up to your right, through a gate and a stile in the hedgerow.

To your right, looking under the bridge, you can see the platforms of what used to be Coalport (West) Station.

6. Continue walking downhill to your left. The path dips through Preen's Eddy picnic area before emerging on the road by Coalport Bridge. Cross the first part of the bridge. Take the track to your left before the second bridge. Follow the path straight on, until it emerges at the Brewery Inn, once owned by the china works. Nice views of the river from the beer terrace.

7. Follow the road until you see the signs on the left pointing to the Coalport China Museum.

A cottage industry making crude earthenware products had been well established in Jackfield before 1700. Broseley specialised in clay pipes and from 1775 fine porcelain had been made at nearby Caughley. This may seem a remote spot for a fine china works, but coal and fireclay could be found locally and china clay imported from Cornwall via the Severn. River transport was much more suited to the distribution of delicate finished products than the rutted, muddy roads.

When Coalport joined forces with Caughley it was 'probably the largest and most expensive porcelain-producing estate in Great Britain' In 1851 there were 500 employees at this factory. Young Thomas Minton was amongst the apprentices. It is claimed, he designed the Willow

Pattern before seeking fame and fortune in the Potteries.

8. Take the path along the roadside, past The Shakespeare, and on to the canal bridge.

To conquer new markets, the iron and coal industries of East Shropshire needed lower transport costs and improved access to the Severn. Elsewhere the answer was canals. Here, said Telford, a canal would have to be "carried over high and rugged ground, along banks of slipping loam, over old coal mines and over where coal mines and iron stone are worked... there is scarcely any ground so difficult". Locks would have been too expensive and restrictive for the heavy traffic. Reynolds' solution was a canal-cum-roller-coaster: a canal with three inclined planes. "They were a source of interest to visitors and, sometimes of excitement .... as when at the Hay, on the chain snapping we have

known a canal boat with five tons of iron pigs on board gain such velocity that on coming in contact with the water on the lower canal (where you are standing) it has broken away from the iron chains which held it to the carriage, bounded in the air, clearing two other boats moored on the side, together with the embankment, and alighted in the Severn, close to the ferry-boat, into which it pitched some of the iron pigs it contained."

Face back the way you have come and go down the steps to your right.

Look up the Hay Inclined Plane, the most spectacular and best preserved in Britain, a 207 feet drop over 350 yards of track. In an hour the incline could take six boats in either direction. Behind you three quarters of a mile of canal, filled with tub-boats, led past warehouses and wharves to Coalport Harbour, where seven inclined planes, rising and falling with the height of the Severn, were used to transfer the coal, pig, sheet and bar iron to barges or trows.

Do not be deceived by the showcases of the museum and the relative peace of this spot. Reynolds' scheme was for

An 1803 diagram of an inclined plane

an 18th century New Town. The new village, soon known as Coalport, with a huge transit warehouse spanning the canal and built out over the river, attracted three potteries, a timber yard producing tub-boats, two chain works and a rope factory making winding ropes and chains for the mines. Not a bad return from "a very rugged, uncultivated bank, which scarcely produced even grass." He also planned an integrated chemical works to make soap, dyes, fertilisers, glass and white lead on the sloping ground above you, so "the minerals may go upon their own legs from one process to another." Financially, according to his intended partner, it promised to "make a dozen of the largest fortunes ever made in Britain." Reynolds' death killed off this would-be Shropshire ICI.

9. Round the edge of the buildings behind you is the Tar Tunnel.

Early visitors compared the Tunnel's dark depths to Hades. It must have seemed the luck of the devil when, digging a drainage canal for the Blists Hill mines, Reynolds and his partners struck it rich right here in Coalport. 300 yards into the hill they found a spring of natural bitumen. The 'Native Tar Concern' was established selling Betton's British Oil for medicinal purposes, as well as barrels of tar or pitch.

10. Take the War Memorial foot-

bridge over the Severn. On the far bank go right along the road to Maws Craft Centre.

When George and Arthur Maw transferred the ailing Worcester Tileries to Benthall in 1852, were they counting on the luck of the Gorge to transform its fortunes? If so it worked, by 1883 success forced them to relocate to this 'new and spacious works'.

What you see today is less than a third of the once-mighty works. Seven bottle kilns, burning 140 tons of coal every few days, and five tall chimneys laid a permanent pall of smoke over the town. The largest encaustic tile works in the world, Maws produced millions of decorative floor and wall tiles for London tube stations, Indian palaces or butchers' shops.

11. Leave Maws and continue along the road before forking right towards the Half Moon pub. Where the road swings right to the pub, continue straight on, following the river path.

Before a towpath for horses was constructed in 1796, gangs of twelve to twenty men would 'bow haul' the trows up the river. Men who lived off the land, stealing sheep and game from the fields and woods near the river. " wherein do they differ from the laborious brutes? ...If there is any difference it consists in this: horses

A cottage made derelict by landslip in 1952

12. The path emerges on to a lane, which leads to St Mary the Virgin, a Victorian church with a fairytale spire, in striking local bricks.

Boatmen once enjoyed Bed & Bawd at *The Severn Trow* opposite the church. In addition to the boatmen's dormitory, there were brothel cubicles, one of which has been retained. Today, rescued from dereliction, it's a high class Bed & Breakfast.

The Severn Trow, The Tumbling Sailors, The Boat were all pubs when Jackfield was the busy port for Coalbrookdale and Ironbridge. Home to watermen, bow-haulers, horse drivers and barge owners, much of this old port was lost when the railway killed off the river traffic.

13. Return to the Tile Museum and your car.

are indulged with a collar to save their breasts, and these, as if theirs were not worth saving, draw without one";

You may detect the odd fruit tree or buddleia along this stretch. They are all that remain of over fifty houses and the main road which were uprooted by the flooding and subsidence of the disused clay. It was one of Keith Waterhouse's, author of Billy Liar, first features for The Daily Mirror. "The almighty crack, a sickening, tearing wrench as a wall comes apart and the guts fall from your cottage. That is the Jackfield Crack. It is the death rattle of a village home." The Guardian said it might be a Poe Story, The Fall Of The Village of Usher.

GRINSHILL

OS Map 1:50,000 Sheet 126, Starting point GR: 505 237

Distance 4½ miles

The story of Grinshill stone is the story of money.
Whether it was to the church in the Middle Ages, prosperous agricultural
estates or engineering projects of the Industrial Revolution, Grinshill stone
gravitated towards wealth. Pieces of Grinshill can be seen all over England:
in the imposing public buildings of Victorian cities, libraries, railway
stations and seaside resorts and even to nineteenth century America.

The walk takes you from Yorton Station to Clive village, the ancestral home of Clive of India, via a copper mine and a magnificent view of the north Shropshire plain to Grinshill quarries. The return journey takes in the varied sandstones of Grinshill village and the magnificent country estates born of agriculture and quarrying.

1. Park at Yorton Station.

At the time the LNWR reached Yorton Baron Haussman was remodelling Paris on an unprecedented scale. In London, John Nash had driven Regent Street through the congested city centre. The railway expanded the market for Grinshill stone beyond Shropshire to the booming manufacturing centres of north and central England, across to the North Wales resort towns to London and even to the States. Shrewsbury was the first of many

stations, including Crewe, Chester, Gloucester and Cheltenham, using Grinshill stone to demonstrate superiority over rival railway companies. Yorton station enabled Grinshill stone to participate in the great building projects of Victorian Britain: according to popular belief, it even upholds the door to 10 Downing Street.

Come out of the station car park and turn right to Yorton Farm on your left.

Until the mid-nineteenth century Grinshill stone was used almost exclusively in the Shrewsbury area and the growing East Shropshire coalfield. Broad-wheeled carts prevented the heavy loads sinking into the mud, and, wherever possible, it was transported by water. Lord Hill's Column, Shrewsbury, contains a 1000 tons of Grinshill, making it the tallest Doric column in the world.

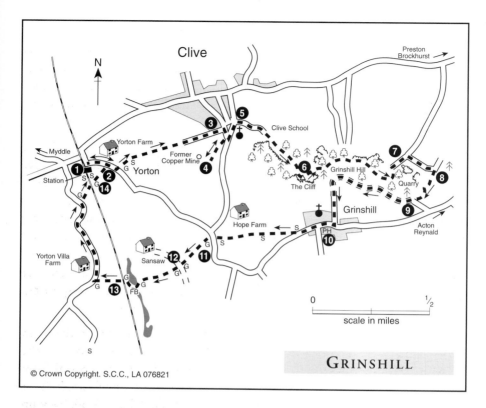

© Crown Copyright. S.C.C., LA 076821

GRINSHILL

The railway took Grinshill stone all over Britain, but it made it too pricey for the local market. Following the opening of Yorton Station in 1858, Shropshire's finest Grinshill buildings had been completed and it was used largely as a dressing stone, as in the doorway to Yorton Farm.

2. The footpath leaves the road at the first farm gate on your left after Yorton Farm.

This track would have been used by the carters and their teams of shires bringing stone down from the hill to the stoneyard next to Yorton station. The finest Grinshill white stone was carved for delicate window tracery, or dressed for facing, while the tougher Flagstone was taken away in the shape of hearths, mantlepieces, fireplaces, flagstones, engine beds, tombstones and gravestones.

Go through the gate and walk straight ahead of you to a stile on the opposite field boundary. Head for the far left-hand corner of the next field and go through the left of two farm gates. The path leads through a tunnel of two hedges and emerges on a metalled track. Continue straight on to the T-junction in Clive.

Clive is the ancestral home of Robert Clive. His own branch of the family were modest Shropshire squires with continual money problems. Clive's Indian conquests made him an eighteenth century millionaire and brought to Britain immense wealth which would help fuel and sustain the Industrial Revolution.

3. Go right and continue downhill until you see a track leading up to the right. Walk up the track past Mine House and a row of cottages to a field gate at the end of the track.

In the field immediately on your right is a mound of earth capped with a ventilation shaft. This was once Clive copper mine. The well in front of Mine House housed a steam engine to operate pumps in the shaft. Altogether 200,000 tons of rock were removed from this bank, producing 200 tons of copper. A narrow path

leading off to the left of the track will take you through a sandstone tunnel to numerous fenced off depressions in the hillside. These were once hand-picked mines probably worked by farm-hands laid off in winter.

Following centuries of this small scale copper mining, The Clive Copper Mining Co. was formed in 1862. Three years later shareholders from Birmingham bought the lease for £4,000. These ventures were always risky and in this case "did no good". The copper deposit quickly ran out and despite desperate prospecting, was not rediscovered.

4. Make your way back to the main road through Clive, nose at the ready to catch a savoury whiff from Blackhurst's traditional smokery at the top of the village. Walk back up the road and through the first gate into the churchyard.

Grinshill stone was always drawn towards money. In the Middle Ages this meant the church. Massive blocks were hauled along tracks, across fields, then floated down the Roden, Tern and Severn to build the twelfth century Abbey at Buildwas. Churches at Wem, Market Drayton, Shawbury and Shrewsbury were

Mine House

all built of Grinshill stone. It carves easily when first quarried, then hardens on exposure to the atmosphere - perfect for intricate carving or engraving headstones. Notice the carved female saints supporting the roof (while the men adorn the stained glass). Another of Clive's famous sons, William Wycherley, the bawdy Restoration dramatist and author of The Country Wife, is buried here in Clive churchyard.

5. Walk through the churchyard following a path past the front of the church and continuing straight on, through a gate onto a narrow woodland path. Follow the path a short distance to a heavily worn sandstone track. Go right along the track. Pass Clive School and Ivy Cottage on your left, then take a path to your right, following a line of telegraph poles gently uphill to a trig-point marking the summit.

From this promontory you can see right across the North Shropshire plain. The commercial success of Grinshill stone was due to more than its quality. The quarries' location on a lowland plain meant it could be extracted and transported economically. In addition the agricultural wealth of North Shropshire provided a ready market for stone manor houses to adorn the prosperous farms and large estates.

6. Walk off the promontory and take the left hand of two paths leading off to the right. The path winds downhill. Go right at the first fork. Keep to the main path to lead you back onto the sandstone track. Go right, passing several sandstone cottages, to the only remaining active quarry.

The cottages are built of Grinshill 'Red'. Red sandstone is relatively common in Shropshire. It weathers less well, will not support delicate masonry, and is less strong than Grinshill 'White'. Since it is also far less expensive, it was the perfect material for quarryworkers' cottages.

Peer through the wooden fence to glimpse modern quarrying in action. The stone is still used in building, including many bridges in Telford, restoration and landscape architecture. The gentle gradients, in marked contrast to the sheer faces of earlier quarries, allow machinery to be driven to the quarry floor.

7. Go right along the sandstone track. When you reach the car park walk behind the interpretative sign to follow the sunken path right around the outside edge of the car park. The path descends. Stop at a fork in the path. Ahead of you is a low wooden post numbered "3".

The Shrewsbury Chronicle 1773 reported that "On Tuesday last was brought from Grinsell Quarry, a key stone for the centre arch of the new bridge, which weigh'd ten tons, eight hundred and forty six pounds, and was drawn by twelve horses".

Grinshill had won the contract for the county's great bridge building programme. This part of the hill has since been known as Bridge Quarries. The stone's strength and resistance to water erosion made it particularly suitable for engineering like the Chirk Aqueduct and the Elan Valley Waterworks for Birmingham.

Go right. On your left is a cutting. Rubble from the quarries would be wheelbarrowed along this cutting then tipped down the hillside. Continuing on the main path, a few yards on from the cutting, you will come to a fork. Go right to "4" on the numbered trail. A short path leads you to a sheer quarry face.

Only a small proportion of this quarry face is the white sandstone for which Grinshill was famous. The face is capped by two metres of mudstone or "overburden" which had to be removed before quarrying could start. Beneath this are nine metres of flagstone and hard burr. The black flecks in this rock made it unsuitable for facework. It was used locally for hearth stones, brick, roofing slates and foundations like that of

William Hazeldine's Paper Mill (see Shrewsbury walk). Beneath the hard burr lies the mother lode: some seven metres of Grinshill White sandstone. At today's prices nearly a billion pounds worth of this stone has been removed from Bridge Quarries alone.

Among the highway engineers to the Shropshire County Trustees for Bridge Construction was the young Thomas Telford. Mastermasons, engineers and famous architects like John Nash, who built Attingham, Cronkhill and Longner Halls from Grinshill stone, would all have climbed up the hill to examine the beds from which their stone would be quarried.

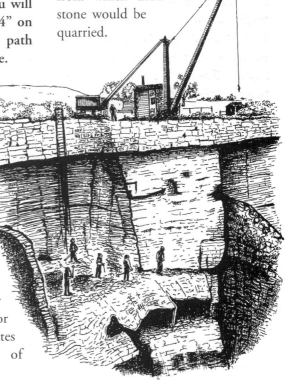

Peer over a wall to the right of the quarry face to look into the abyss of one of Grinshill's deepest quarries, undisturbed for over a hundred and fifty years.

Despite the depth of this quarry, it was not until 1880 that a steam crane was installed. Large scale blocks were at a premium and the stone was hauled out using pulleys attached to oak beams wedged into the corners of the quarry. Steam-driven channelling and dressing were also tested but never adopted. Traditional methods were thought to bring least harm to the precious stone and changed little from the days of William Quarriator, a thirteenth century Grinshill quarryman.

Herringbone marks from quarrymen's picks can be seen on the quarry face. When the over-burden, flag rock and hard burr had been removed, the surface of the 'White' stone was carefully marked into rectangles. The quarrymen then cut around the blocks using double headed 'jad picks' to make grooves nine to twelve inches wide and three to four feet deep. Wedges were inserted into the grooves, or 'gutters', around each block and manipulated until the block was freed from the bedrock.

8. Walk back to the main path and continue right. The steps leading up to the left of the path lead to a manager's office from which the labour force and output could be surveyed.

Initially Grinshill quarries were divided into three. Bridge Quarries were owned by Lord Hill. During the period of Shropshire bridge-building, the lessee was Martha Walford, daughter of a famous quarrying family. The first dated reference to the quarries was 1769 when she was hauled before the bailiffs in Shrewsbury, accused of delaying work on the English Bridge. Contrary to accepted business practice, she had taken downpayments on all stone removed from the quarries from a contractor in The Strand. The Corbets owned part of the hill, which they had leased to the Cureton family since the Middle Ages. In the nineteenth century they also acquired Bridge Quarries and formed the Bridge and Cureton Co. The third share was owned by the Kilverts, who had worked the stone in the 1600's and re-opened the quarries in the nineteenth century. All three companies united when John Kilvert retired in 1908.

Continue downhill. You will see a track coming in from the left.

The stones set into each side of the track were used to stop the heavily-laden carts sinking into the mud.

9. Continue straight on until you come to a house and a fork in the

track. Go left, then left again on the main track into Grinshill village.

As you walk through the village you will see many examples of Grinshill sandstone. Grinshill 'White' Stone comes in pink, yellow and grey, but it was the palest stone which became fashionable in the eighteenth century well-suited to the restrained architectural style.

In the village go right along the road. Just outside the village, on your right, is a way-marked stile. Cross the stile and head diagonally left across the field to a stile beneath a tall ash tree. Head for a gate to the left of the oak in the centre of the field and just to the left of the black and white manor. Go through the gate and cross the next field to a stile straight ahead. Go over the stile and onto the road.

11. Cross the road to a public footpath opposite. Go through the left-hand of two gates and walk up the right-hand side of the field. Go through a gate onto a driveway. You can see a large country house up to your right.

12. Cross the drive to a farm gate. Go through the farm gate and follow the right-hand boundary to a kissing gate on the opposite boundary. Go through the kissing gate. Continue following the right-hand boundary to a gate beside a lake on your left. Go through the gate and follow the

track over a footbridge and through a kissing gate, The path veers immediately left through a gate and a stile. You will see a step-ladder on your right. Climb the stepladder and walk up to the railway-line.

Without lingering unduly, notice that this section of track is unusually straight - so straight that it was used to test the high speed performance of new trains.

13. Cross the track and climb over a second step-ladder. Keep to the right-hand field boundary. Go through a gate in the opposite boundary onto the road and turn right. On the right, just after the road twists around the church, is a farm gate with way-marker. Go through the gate and walk straight across the field to a stile on the opposite boundary. Follow the path over the railway track, down a flight of steps and over a stile.

14. Go through a gate and follow the field boundary to a farm gate opposite Yorton Farm. Walk onto the road and go left back to the station.

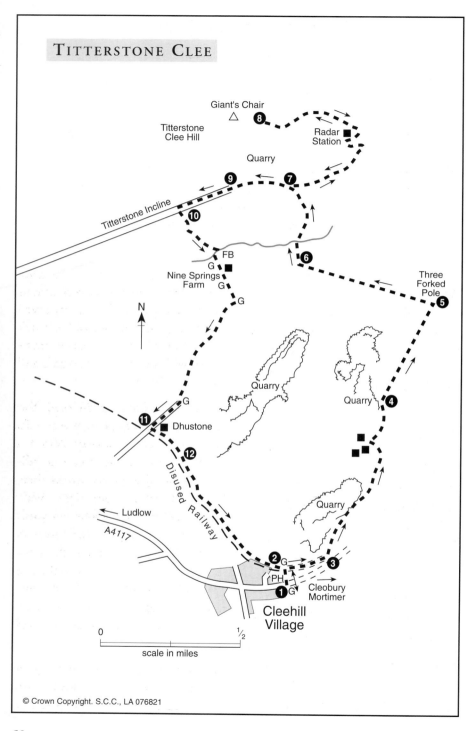

TITTERSTONE CLEE

Giant's Chair

Titterstone
Clee Hill

Radar
Station

Quarry

Titterstone Incline

Three
Forked
Pole

FB

Nine Springs
Farm

N

Quarry

Quarry

Dhustone

Disused Railway

Ludlow

A4117

Quarry

PH

Cleobury
Mortimer

Cleehill
Village

0   ½

scale in miles

© Crown Copyright. S.C.C., LA 076821

58

TITTERSTONE CLEE

OS Map 1:50,000 sheet 137, Starting point GR: 595 754
Distance 5 miles

Today the Clee Hills are a secluded highland spot for hikers from all over the Midlands. Less than a hundred years ago Brown Clee was the highest coal mine in England, while on Titterstone, railways, inclined planes, ropeways and two thousand employees converged to extract dhustone - the roadstone which paved the highways and city streets of industrial Britain.

1. Park on the Ludlow Road (A4117) opposite the Victoria Inn, in Cleehill village. Cross the road and go up a track to the right of the pub. Go through a farm gate. Just before the track veers right, peer over the small gate on your left.

From here you can look down the broad grassy track which brought the Great Western Railway to Cleehill. Within a year of the railway's arrival, labour came from Scotland, Wales and Ireland and between 1500 and 2000 men were working these hills. Wagons of corn, meal and barrels of stout arrived to feed the growing population. But the wagons returned without the coal that the GWR had anticipated. It was needed here on the hills to fuel an entirely new industry.

2. Follow the track round to the right. It emerges on a metalled road.

Craven Place, the building on your right, was the office for the quarries. This road was once a network of rails with the capacity for twenty-seven railway trucks. This was only a small portion of the daily mineral trains loaded with stone to lay the roads and railways of Britain.

3. Go left, walking up the road. You pass a lake-filled quarry on your left, formally a marble quarry. About a third of a mile up the road, immediately before the quarry works there is a track off to your right. Walk down the track for about ten yards until you see a way-marked footpath on the right. Follow the path into a dell, past a cottage on your right and straight on uphill. Head for the two humps on top of the hill. The path leads between them and hits a broad grassy track.

Turn left along the track, passing an abandoned animal enclosure on your right. When you reach a

crumbling metalled track go left again until you see a way-marked footpath on the left. Take the footpath across the heathland toward a cluster of slag heaps, patchily covered in grass.

Until the 1850s the Clee Hills' primary industry was coal. The mines were the highest in England. Transportation was costly and primitive, falling to packhorses or, more often, women:

"Fine and handsome upstanding wenches they were and well dressed too," recalled one visitor to the Titterstone Wake in 1846, "but you wouldna' know 'em the next day with a bag of coal strapped on their backs…"

But the coal itself was hard and bright and demand had grown with the Midland industries. Telford drew up plans to create a canal link to the Severn, but the hills would have to await God's Wonderful Railway before they would be united with industrial Britain.

4. On the horizon you will see a pole with three prongs. Head for the pole.

Many of the miners and quarrymen travelled from neighbouring villages, Ludlow, Cleobury Mortimer or even Leominster. The working day began at 6 am. Following ten hours work they would make the return journey

across these hills. In fog or early morning darkness walking through a maze of pit shafts and quarries was extremely hazardous. The Three Forked Pole has been used as a landmark for many centuries. The men would also leave trails of broken crockery known as 'pitchuk' to illuminate the paths.

5. At the pole walk left. The path passes beside an active quarry to the left.

This was the first major Dhustone quarry. Locally the stone was renowned for its exceptional strength and had been used for hundreds of

The Three Forked Pole

years in building. In the late 1850s a Mr Clarke was appointed by the GWR to build the spur from Ludlow via Bitterley to Dhustone village and on to Craven Place. The railway was designed to transport coal. Mr Clarke used local expertise and materials. Clee Hill dhustone was put to use in retaining walls, bridges, loading wharfs and the foundation of the railway. Mr Clarke became convinced that the stone could not be equalled for strength. When he was asked to build the docks at Cardiff, he agreed only on the condition that he use Clee Hill stone.

He leased a mile and a half of hill from Limer's Gate. Now that the railway had arrived, there was nothing to stop Dhustone paving the roads of industrial Britain.

6. The path follows a rubble-filled water course downhill. To your right you can see the giant golf-balls of Titterstone Radar Station. Straight ahead a fence runs across your path. Walk right following the fence as it turns downhill and comes out on the road next to a cattle-grid.

7. This was once known as Limer's Lane because it led across Clee Hill to Oreton Limeworks. Go right along the metalled road. The road leads to the Radar station. A short continuation from the end of the road and across the grassy upland will reward you with a pause upon the Giant's Chair and a vast Shropshire view.

8. Return from the land of legend back to the hard realities of the rock face, by turning into the lower quarry, now a car park.

From the day of Mr Clarke's first explorations, there was a great demand for Clee Hill stone. Although in the 1860s road transport still took second place to railways, there was a move to improve road links between stations and in town centres.

Dhustone remained the yardstick of stone's well into the age of the car. To cope with increased demand, a third quarry company, Field and Mackay opened these quarries in 1881 and 1911. They are over 1500 feet above sea level, exposed to frost and especially dangerous. Titterstone Clee was formed when a fiery stream of lava erupted and then rapidly cooled leaving tiny fissures in the rock. At night the quarrymen lit fires beneath the rockface to expand these fissures and crack the rock. No-one wore protective headgear, and one member of each gang kept a constant watch for any rock movement. When boulders fell they shattered anything in their path. Many quarrymen were killed by flying splinters or rock falls.

When the stone had been dislodged it was broken with 28lb 'bolsters' (13 kilo hammers), then loaded into trucks using a "reek un pon" (rake and pan). The loaded pans weighed about 25 kilos, so heavy that during the Second World War Italian and German prisoners insisted on lifting them in pairs.

Walk down one of the steep paths leading to the abandoned quarry works just below the car-park.

From the face the trucks were hauled by horses to a small locomotive which took them to the stone-crushers or sett-makers. The sett-makers craft lasted from Mr Clarke's first experiments until the 1950s, long after it had died out elsewhere in Britain. The men took the rough stones onto their knees and hammered them into near-perfect cubes. At the beginning of the century two new stone 'crackers' were brought in. The great concrete containers on stilts are the remains of stone crushers. After being crushed the stone gravitated through sorting

screens, then passed down a chute into wheel-barrows either to be broken further or to be sent down the railway incline. The stone dust, initially a waste product and the cause of lung problems, was later used to construct the water pipes from the Rhayader Dams to Birmingham.

9. Walk towards the far end of this lower quarry until you see a sign to 'The Shropshire Way' pointing down the hill.

This steep path was a self-acting incline over a mile in length. The wagons slid downhill to Bitterley Wharf where they tipped into mineral trains.

On the other side of Clee Hill, at Catherton, the stone had to pass over bogs, woods, roads and rivers before reaching a railway. The solution was to build one of the longest and most remarkable ropeways in Britain. The rope was seven miles in length,

weighed 35 tons and was suspended on 55 trestles. Buckets of stone weighing 10 hundredweight were carried through the air, $3^1/_2$ miles to the Ditton Priors Light Railway.

Follow the incline downhill, until you see a path passing under the incline, again following the signs for 'The Shropshire Way'.

10. Come off the incline and follow the path left. The path crosses a track, runs over a footbridge and up to a stile. Cross the stile and walk up the left-hand side of the field. Go through the gate in the left-hand corner of the field into a farmyard. Continue straight on through the farmyard along a track. Keep to the track until you emerge on the road. Go left down the road to the terrace of houses.

This terrace was built for quarrymen by the Rouse Boughtons, just one of the estate owners who were paid royalties for quarrying on their land.

11. Continue down the road and take the third track on your left, Railway Terrace. Pass the blue brick station master's house on your right and go through a small gate at the end of the terrace. Walk straight on to a wide track. Follow the track to a stone and brick wall on your left.

Dhustone came down the hill and was lowered from the wall into trucks. The original dhustone setts can be seen at the bottom of the wall. Later brick was added and the wall is crowned by concrete towers. Mr Clarke's Dhustone to Bitterley incline ran from here. It had three rails with a turn-out of four rails halfway down the hill. This allowed the descending full trucks to pass the empty trucks, reducing both the cost and the width of the line.

12. Follow the old railway track until you reach a cross-roads. Continue straight ahead, walking behind a row of modern houses. Go through a gate onto another track.

The large warehouse ahead of you was the Clee Hill Transport and Rolling Company which ran the first road rollers in the area. A little way up the hill was the site of the first Clee Hill tarmacadam plant, built about the time of the First World War. Until more sophisticated plants were built, rivers of burning tarmacadam would often be seen pouring down the hillside from the factory.

New techniques of road building would bring an end to Clee Hill's reign as king of the roads. Reinforcements have made strength less important in construction. Dhustone's remarkable resistance can even be a disadvantage, since softer stones break down to form smoother surfaces. While the radar station uses state-of-the-art technology to scour the airspace above the Clee Hills, the quarrying industry is hampered by the same problems of transportation it faced over a hundred years ago. Road haulage is expensive. Without the railway, only a local market remains viable. The "superb road-stone" can only be sold within a thirty mile radius of the hill.

Turn right along the track, passing the pub and crossing the main road to the car.

Note. Lubberland - an unmissable mining landscape is only a few minutes away. Lubberland is a series of mini volcanoes created by coal mining. The circular mounds are spoil and the central depressions result from collapsed mine shafts. These bell-pits were mined at least until the Second World War. They are brilliantly preserved and are perfect terrain for an archaeological scramble.

Directions - Take the Cleobury Mortimer to Cleehill road (A4117). Just east of Doddington take the road to Oreton. Pull over at the bus stop opposite a turning for Stock Hall. Walk across the scrub in the direction of the radar domes. After 75 yards you will find yourself standing amid the bell-pits.

CHURCH STRETTON

OS Map 1:50,000 Sheet No. 126, Starting point GR: 433 955

Distance: 4 miles

Church Stretton had certain advantages in the fight for the excursionist's penny: hills, water and most importantly the railway. But the development of its primary industry, leisure and tourism, was never a matter of chance. From the early days it was a few individuals, a vicar, a postmaster and their supporters, who proclaimed Stretton to be a "Little Switzerland - without the wolves or avalanches". Their foresight seems uncanny as the 1980's and 90's have seen towns all over Britain fighting a battle which was fought in Church Stretton a hundred years before.

Their efforts have left a lasting impression on the town. Benches, country walks, roads, houses and the golf links make Church Stretton what it is today- a town which draws its wealth from day-trippers, holiday-makers, walkers and the thousands who have come here to retire - in short the leisure industry.

1. Park in the upper car park of the Cardingmill Valley, just beyond the tea-rooms.

By the latter part of the nineteenth century, Church Stretton was already becoming a popular resort with Victorian excursionists. With the growth of cities, the middle classes sought the country. While the working classes toiled in conditions which necessitated the suppression of finer feelings, middle class literature made a cult of the Romantic sensibility.

The waterfall which lies just up the valley to your right, was the destination of many a Victorian seeking dramatic natural beauty. Even this car park is testimony to the popularity of the valley. If you look carefully you will find a sign and steps revealing its former use - as a swimming pool.

Walk down the valley until you reach the three-storey brick building on your right.

This was the carding mill from which the valley took its name. Initially its sole purpose was the combing of fleece. Despite the installation of spinning jennies and looms, the scale of business was too small to compete with the northern factories. The mill limped along for a further fifty years before a sale notice of 1870 suggested making use of the waters, to open

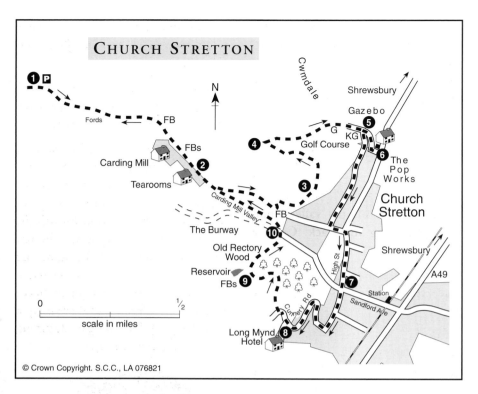

"a hydropathic institute or brewery".

Church Stretton water is renowned for purity. The pre-Cambrian rock from which it springs gives it an enviably low mineral content - perfect for a brewery or a Victorian health farm. By 1881 the Stretton Hills Aerated Water Company had re-opened the Mill for the production of soda water, ginger beer and cups of tea, served in "a large tearoom for the accommodation of visitors to the hills". The twin industries of Church Stretton - water and tourism were born.

2. **Pass the Chalet Pavillion Tea Room on your right and continue** down the valley until you see a bench on the right. Almost immediately opposite a narrow path climbs up from the valley floor. Take this path. Continue as it swings left and follows a fence on the right. Ignoring a gate on your right, go through a second gate straight ahead of you onto a track.

3. Keep following the fence on your right until you meet a track descending from the left. Head left up the track and at a fork go left again. The track heads up the fairway between two hill-tops, so beware flying golfballs. When you come to the 3rd green, at the top of

the hill, leave the track to the right. Walk to the left of the 3rd green to meet a narrow path heading down the left hand side of the valley immediately in front of you.

4. At the head of the valley U-turn and follow the brooklet down the valley floor. The path meets a farm gate. Go through the gate and continue straight on downhill to a gravelled track on the valley floor. Go right along the track. Cross a cattle grid.

5. Continue a little further and you will notice a gazebo to the left of the track.

In 1883 the Stretton Hills Mineral Water Company opened a purpose built bottling plant. Beneath the gazebo lies the glazed brick Victorian reservoir, which still supplies the world with waters from the Cwm Dale spring. This competition proved too much for the Church Stretton Aerated Water Company, "sole lessees of the celebrated Long Mynd Spring" and by the early 1900's their warehouse had been given over to supplying tourists with yet more tea. The Stretton Hills Company, however, was acquired by Jewsbury & Brown Ltd and "stood head and shoulders above other manufacturers of table waters". Queen Victoria decreed that the governors of the colonies should enjoy a supply. Stretton Water was sipped at tables throughout the Empire.

Continue along the track to the road and go left to the tap and plaque on the wall in front of the factory.

Francis Sutton F.C.S., F.I.C. was an eminent chemist. The waters were equally extolled for the treatment of influenza, sleeplessness, sluggish livers, gout, rheumatism, bronchitis, catarrh, weak digestion, obesity, anaemia and all round ill-health. The cure was of course most effective when taken with a draught of clean, bracing Stretton air and therein lay a new lease of life for the declining agricultural community.

6. Retrace your steps up the track to a bench on your left. Just after the bench is a sort of kissing gate. Go left through the gate and follow the path along the edge of a wood. The path emerges in a side road. Continue straight on. At the T-junction turn left, then right on the main road. Stop at the cross roads in the centre of the town.

In 1884 the Severn Tunnel opened. Church Stretton was now on the main railway line from South Wales and the West Country to Merseyside, Manchester, Leeds and Scotland. Two weeks later, the Reverend Holland Sandford called a meeting of notables. Drawing on the splendours of the Champs Elysees, the Reverend asked for their support in planting an avenue of lime trees from the station to The Hotel. After many more discussions and disagreements, the first trees were planted on December 19th 1884, by George Prees, who lived in the house where Lloyds Bank now stands. Only days after the ceremony many of the trees had been slashed. Although the culprits were never caught, it is easy to imagine their motivation. How were those who ended their lives in the workhouse to benefit from such a cosmetic approach to the local economy? What about the traditional industries of agriculture and wool? What about housing and poor relief? Add a little jealousy and conservatism and the Reverend had a powerful opponent.

One man who was unfailing in his support, was the secretary to the Sandford Avenue Tree Planting Scheme, George Reginald Windsor. George Windsor ran the post office now the shop on the corner of Burway Road. He also wrote a guidebook, which he distributed free of charge, to railway waiting rooms throughout the country and instigated, edited and sold "The Church Stretton Times and Visitors List", a local newspaper whose first editorial was headed simply "Sell Stretton".

7. Continue straight ahead between the Lloyds and Midland Bank buildings into High Street. After about a third of a mile go right up Cunnery Road.

In 1885 a second committee was formed with the intention of "further improving the approaches to the town of Church Stretton". During the following twenty years, the Stretton Land Company and the Stretton Building Company built roads like this one into the surrounding hillsides. They sold building plots. Houses like Woodcote (on your left) were built in the fashionable neo-half-timbered style that Pevsner calls "the hallmark of Church Stretton".

Continue up the road until you reach the gates to the Longmynd Hotel.

A "Hydro" was seen as a further step in putting Stretton on the map. Little matter that the nearest saline waters were at Wentnor and would have to be pumped over the Long Mynd, Church Stretton was to become a Spa. A company was found to undertake the construction and deliver the water to a pump room in the town. Meanwhile the railway would bring water from Llandrindod Wells.

In 1900 these gates opened on the Church Stretton Hydropathic Establishment. The end of the nineteenth century had seen a boom in the town's development as a resort. The cure involved wrapping in wet linen sheets and showering in ice-cold water. Hydropathy was the invention of Priestnitz, an Austrian to rival Sacher Masoch. Not surprisingly, in Britain the fashion was short-lived and the Hydro's strict rules about food, smoke, snuff and alcohol were soon replaced by the comfort and luxury of the Long Mynd Hotel. As for the vision of Church Stretton the spa town? - it so nearly succeeded, but at the last moment the plans to pump water from Wentnor collapsed, rendering the Reverend Sandford's grand design a literal pipe-dream.

8. Almost directly opposite the gates, on the other side of the road is a car park. Walk down through the car park to a kissing gate. Follow the path straight up hill to the left of a large sycamore immediately in front of you. At the top of the hill go through a second kissing gate into the Rectory Wood.

This was one of many walks laid out by the Church Stretton Advancement Association in emulation of Continental spas. It was recently turned into a nature trail by Shropshire Conservation Trust. Others include the Lovers' Walk running from the Pop Works, and the path across the golf links.

Pass a wooden post numbered 7 on the trail and head straight downhill through the wood. The path then swings left to join another path running parallel to the valley. Go left along this path, passing no.5, then leading downhill and over a brook. Pass no.4 and go through a kissing gate. Walk uphill toward a sluice and the old town reservoir. Take the path leading sharply right in the direction of the Burway.

Just before the path emerges on the road, you reach a wrought iron bench. If you look at the plaque you may just be able to make out the words "Church Stretton Advancement Association 1908", yet another legacy of Sandford and his followers.

10. Cross the road (The Burway) and go down the track immediately opposite.

The Rowans, on your right, is an

inspiring example of the building which took place in Church Stretton at the end of the last century. Built into the hillside, with a large balcony it emphasises the improvers' claim that Church Stretton was a little Switzerland, minus the avalanches and wolves.

13. Follow the footpath until you emerge on the main route through the valley. Continue past the Chalet Pavilion Tea Rooms, (built in 1920 and still serving fruit scones and sponge cake) back to the car-park.

Stretton Hills Mineral Water Co. - bottling plant

EXPLORING SHROPSHIRE
with Shropshire Books

BOOKS

Available Now

UNDISCOVERED SHROPSHIRE
14 Walks in North Shropshire
Eve Powell

WALKS WITH WRITERS
Gordon Dickins and
Gladys Mary Coles

GREEN WALKS FROM
OSWESTRY
Mary Hignett

WALKS AROUND TELFORD
David Gregory

TEN WALKS THAT CHANGED
THE WORLD
Walks into Shropshire's Industrial Past
Kate and Keith Pybus

Forthcoming

WALKS AROUND BRIDGNORTH
Gillian Mortimer

TOWN TRAILS

Available Now

Bridgnorth
Ludlow

Forthcoming

Much Wenlock

LEAFLETS

Available Now

Acton Scott
Alveley
Ludlow
Market Drayton
Much Wenlock
Stiperstones
Stokesay
The Jack Mytton Way

Forthcoming

Bridgnorth
Cleobury Mortimer

CYCLE TRAILS

Available Now

Corvedale

Countryside and Woodland

The Jack Mytton Way (Long distance
path for horses, cyclists and walkers)

Cycling for Pleasure in the English
Marches

For further details of these and many more books on Shropshire contact:

SHROPSHIRE BOOKS
Information and Community Services,
Column House, 7 London Road
SHREWSBURY SY2 6NW